To: Brenda

Hope you enjoy
our efforts in
the poems and
stories we've created

Ghee de Munnik

A Mariposa Writers'
Group Publication

Canadian Cataloguing in Publication Data

A Canvas of Words, Our Literary Lapses II

ISBN: 978-0-9877862-0-3

1. Adult; 2. Short Stories/Prose/Poetry; 3. Fiction/Non-Fiction;
4. Fantasy; 5. Young Adult; 6. Children:

The Mariposa Writers' Group

Tel:	(705) 327-7846
Email:	mariposawritersgroup@hotmail.ca
	ademunnik@sympatico.ca

Web Address: www.mariposawritersgroup.com

Front Cover:
The Stephen Leacock Boathouse on the grounds of the Stephen Leacock National Historic Site in Orillia, Ontario. With the ducks in the foreground and the abundance of water all around, the scene conveys a tranquility highly conduce to the art of creative writing. Photograph courtesy of Michelle Duff.

A Canvas of Words

Our Literary Lapses II

**Published by The Mariposa
Writers' Group**

Dedicated to struggling writers everywhere who constantly strive to perfect the written craft. May your efforts some day bear fruit.

Write On

ABOUT THE AUTHORS

The **Mariposa Writers' Group** was formed in 1996 by a number of people who wanted to write, share skills and information and have an opportunity to hear their work read. Of course, becoming good enough to be published was everyone's secret dream. The first meeting was held at the home of Marilyn Rumball, who is the only remaining member of the original group. The group has grown both in numbers and in activities and meets monthly at the Reception Centre of the Carson-Doolittle Funeral Home in Orillia. For the past seven years, the group has sponsored prose and poetry competitions for emerging, unpublished adult writers as well as a youth competition for children from grades 3 to 8, all held in conjunction with their mini festival, Lake Country Literary Lapses. This festival is held in August at the Stephen Leacock National Historic Site in Orillia. The day is devoted to a workshop and a gala evening at which the winners of the three competitions are announced. With prize money to third place for all contests and recognition to fifth in the adult contests, these contests become more popular every year. The Festival has grown since its inception with attendance and participation increasing annually. This Anthology is the second for The Mariposa Writers' Group. We hope that you enjoy it.

Members of The Mariposa Writers' Group who contributed to this anthology are: Ted Beaton, George Belajac, Jim Butler, Doreen Caldwell, Frank Daulby, Joan Daulby, Alice de Munnik, Michelle Duff, John Forrest, William J. Gibson, David Green, Muriel Hemmings, Cindy McCarthy, Jacqui Morrison, Anne O'Rourke, Evelyn N. Pollock, Marilyn Rumball, Christine Spear, Margot Strongitharm, Veronica Weller, Janke Wielenga and Tammy Woodrow.

TABLE OF CONTENTS

Name   Page No.

Ted Beaton 12
  A Soldier Still 13
  Strangers to the Boy 19

George Belajac 25
  Tsunami 26
  Dear Grandma and Grandpa 27
  The Chesterfield 28
  Summer Storm 29
  Grandpa's Secret Plan 30

Jim Butler 32
  Moon Landing 33
  Time of Use Hydro Rates 35

Doreen Caldwell 41
  Murray, Moose and Me 42
  The Thornton Chronicles, *"The Great Auctioneer's Daughter"* ... 45

Frank Daulby 49
  Jean and Arlo 50
  The Wedding Dress 56
  Waltz Me to the Edge of Love 63

Joan Daulby 69
  Days of Yesterday, Today and Tomorrow 70
  Miss Dench 75
  Vienna Vanilla 78

Name   Page No.

Alice de Munnik 90
Buster 91
Waiting for the Call An Excerpt from the Memoir, *"Assimilating"*.. 94
The Reluctant Lover 97

Michelle Duff 99
All Save One 100
Toby's Meeting 103
Tracey's Gift 112

John Forrest 114
Dad's Dinghy 115
One of Those Mornings 119
The Coach 122
The Show Must go On 125

William J. Gibson 128
At Cat Island, South Carolina 2002 129
Heard Something in Your Voice 130
Love Poem Number One 132
Love Poem Number Two 133
Red Jack on a Red Queen 134
Care 1979 136
Dutchie Goes Down the Road 1974 139
In the Bar 141
Stanley Park Zoo 142
The Idea of Order on Langton Ave 143
Way Past Midnight 146

Name	Page No.
David Green	148
Fragments	149
Serenade No. 9 (The Posthorn)	152
Muriel Hemmings	153
A Song for Canada	154
Four Tall Poles	155
Guess Who?	156
My Wish for You	157
Objects of Pity	158
Volunteers	160
Cindy McCarthy	162
I Fell From the Sky	163
Montreal Vignette	164
Visit	165
Yellow Butterflies	166
Jacqui Morrison	168
Vignettes of Canada	169
Stained Glass/Shattered Glass	170
Anne O'Rourke	173
And I Never Saw Her Face	174
Life is a Journey	175
Mother Earth	175
Smorgasbord	176

Name   Page No.

Evelyn N. Pollock 178
And All Will Be Well 179
Chance Meeting 186
Rule of Thumb 193

Marilyn Rumball 195
Last Day at Devon 196
New Beginnings 197
The Rats in My Classroom Were Not Always the Kids 198

Christine Spear 200
Lion: A Fantasy (Maybe) 201
Notes from a Condemned House 203

Margot Strongitharm 208
Hugs 209
Ripples 210
The Easter Lilly 211
The Old Oak on the Hill 212

Veronica Weller 213
A Luncheon Rendezvous 214
Go With the Flow 215
Chapters I to VI from, *Scarlett, the Turtle Who Wears Diapers* 216

Janke Wielenga 222
Something Simple 223
Present 224

Name	Page No.

Janke Wielenga (cont.)

Chickadee Theories 225
April Circuit of Strings and Cat Baskets 226
Episode with Birds 227
Kissing Your Two Lips 228
All Summer She Brought in Flowers 230
October Morning 231
After the Leaves Fall 233
Evergreen in Snow Storm 234
January Praise Psalm 235
Winter Ravens in Snowfall 236
Before the News at Six 238
Meningitis 239
O Death, Where is Thy Sting? 240
A Room in February Lamplight 241
The Stupor of Mourning 243
Dusk's Litany 244
The Room 245
Afternoons to Tea 246
Water Closet 248
The Way We Left Her There 249

Tammy Woodrow 252

Chapters One and Two (from the Novel, *Painted Dreams*) 253
A Wind's Embrace 264
The Thoughtful Brush 265

The Stephen Leacock home on the grounds of the Stephen Leacock National Historic Site in Orillia, Ontario. It is on these beautifully kept parklands that The Mariposa Writers' Group holds its annual Lake Country Literary Lapses Festival competition for aspiring writers.

TED BEATON

TED began singing the alphabet at the age of five. The most confusing part was the "elemenopee" section. Even now, more than 40 years later, he still gets confused about whether or not it accounts for one letter or two. The first word he spelled correctly was "A" (although admittedly he sometimes spelled it with an "I".) Full sentences like, "Why?" and "How?" came shortly afterwards. Soon he was writing out two and even three word sentences. The word he uses most is: "Yes", which is a troublesome habit. His favourite word is "orhibulate."

He joined the Mariposa Writers' Group in January of 2010. Since then he has been desperately trying to put words in orders that make sense.

Since his birth, Ted Beaton has been living: something he plans on continuing doing until he dies.

He currently resides in Oro Station with his wife and dog. Both of his entries in this anthology are non-fiction, which is a fancy way of saying true.

A Soldier Still

Picture a soldier marching. Weighted in full kit and carrying a mock weapon, he passes utilitarian military buildings, their boxy shadows receding under a rising spring sun. As he approaches the midway point of his thirteen kilometre trek, the pain comes on in earnest and his ankles begin to seize as if bolts have been driven through them and every step pulls the ratchet tighter. They will loosen in time: after another four or five kilometres, another thirty or forty minutes, hopefully. Until then he will continue his hobbled pace, kicking awkwardly forward. There is no irony in the blister he feels forming. He can't stop again. He's already stopped once to fix a sock, and this is a timed requirement. But they're so tight, and they hurt so badly.

A second soldier marches beside him, urging him along with gentle francophone blasphemies. She is there to see him through this. She is an athlete, a military ironman champion, and a friend. She watches him closely. She can push a soldier through typical discomforts, but his are atypical, and he refuses to complain.

A third soldier follows in a pickup truck, slowly rolling along, reverently anticipating all contingencies. His job is to either document success or aid in the event of failure.

Since Matthew Dicks was old enough to consider such things, a military career had been an option. The events of September 11, 2001 clinched it. He snatched up the last remaining high school credits needed for his diploma and was sworn in on January 24, 2002. On February 7, 2007, he landed in Afghanistan as Corporal Matthew Dicks, a member of the Royal Canadian Dragoons, there with his squad to patrol and reconnoitre aboard a lav-25 Coyote – *Sixty-one Bravo* – a gunner.

Thirty-two days later, his squad was returning to base camp after three days at a forward observation post. It had been a tense day. Their relief struck an improvised explosive device on route to meet them. There were wounded. In heat reaching over forty degrees centigrade, hours were spent assessing risks and situations: whether to move, to assist or to stay put. At dusk, they received orders to return to base.

Corporal Dicks was in the turret atop the Coyote – scanning. A gunner is always scanning. His squad was moving cautiously along hard-packed dirt pathways intersected by *wadis* (large ditches used to carry irrigation water to local crops.) As they entered the third one, Cpl Dicks did what he always did entering a *wadi* – he braced for the bump.

... blackout. Screaming. Voices. His own voice screaming. Blinded. Nothing. There was a call for a fire extinguisher. Why? His legs. They felt on fire. Blackout ....

He opened his eyes to a bright room of solemn faces. Through the fog of pain and morphine, he discovered he was in the Role 3 Medical Center at Kandahar Airfield. Things were explained. Trooper Jesse Renauld, who had been surveying from the back of the vehicle, was thrown meters and was miraculously uninjured. Trooper Patrick Pentland, the driver, and Master Corporal Allen Stewart, who had been sitting in the turret beside Cpl Dicks when they entered the *wadi*, have fallen. It was the morning of their Ramp Ceremony.

The news was devastating to the fractured soldier. Cpl Dicks demanded he be allowed to attend the ceremony and was wheeled out to the airfield on a gurney. He managed a salute as his friends were loaded into a Hercules to begin their journey home over brown earth and blue oceans, where they would be driven in black cars along a grey road lined with red and white flags, where they would be returned to their friends and families, where they would be laid in their graves.

After the ceremony, Cpl Dicks was returned to the hospital – slipping once again out of consciousness. Both physically and emotionally, he was critical.

In and out. Fragments. His right leg was enormous, strapped together with metal rods. All below his waist was hidden under blankets. Information about his injuries was vague and confusing. His head hurt. He couldn't remember things. Nurses changed a wet dressing on his calf. There was no sense of time. In and out. Morphine only dulled the blades. Voices uttered soft commands. There were operations. There were operations to prepare for operations. Triage. In and out. He was being prepared for the move to Germany. Landstuhl. Half way home. Landstuhl is where soldiers get better. In and out. He was loaded onto an airplane and up he went. Barely in the sky he flatlined, and his flight was redirected to Bagram Air Base. He didn't get to Germany. He was still in Afghanistan. In a paranoid jag of fever and morphine he hallucinated. He had fallen into enemy hands. He panicked. They were going to kill him. He pleaded for his release. He fought against them. It took a day to stabilize him and get him back in the air. Out and in. In and out.

Landstuhl Regional Medical Center was where the repair work to his body would begin. The list was long. He had suffered a severe concussion, and there were bones broken in his face. Both ankles were broken (though the fracture in his left one wouldn't be discovered for some weeks.) All the bones in his right leg were smashed. Three of the four main ligaments were torn free on both knees. There were fractures to his second and fifth lumbar vertebrae. There was what was described as a "shrapnel wound" to his right calf – a missing chunk of flesh the volume and shape of a supermarket eggplant. To complicate things, he was infected with *Acinetobacter baumannii*, a multidrug resistant organism that lives in soil and enters the body through open wounds. It is a bug that prospers in places where there is war.

When it was learned his mother had no passport, the problem was seen to by the military. In a feat of unimagined bureaucratic efficiency, she received hers in days. She arrived in Germany with Uncle Wayne, a favourite, to the news that there was a real possibility the patient may yet be counted among the fallen. His will to continue fighting a battle that lasted a mere instant was diminishing. There were moments when it was feared he was giving up. But his mother and uncle's presence proved a needed medicine and their swallowed tears an elixir taken by proxy. The patient's condition improved.

Intermitted by murky periods of recuperation, long operations were performed to reassemble, at least in part, his right leg. When he was healthy enough to return to Canada to a waiting family and anxious friends, the remainder of his surgeries – to repair his ankle, to replace the ligaments in his knees, to graft skin onto his calf – were to take place at Ottawa Civic Hospital over a period of two weeks. There, exploring the extraordinary pain he seemed to be suffering during physiotherapy, the fracture in his left ankle was finally discovered. More surgery.

From Ottawa Civic, he was moved to Pembroke General for recovery and continued physiotherapy. When he was given a wheelchair in preparation for release, a logistical problem suddenly arose. To reach his apartment, Cpl Dicks had to ascend three flights of stairs. There was some discussion about him moving into his off-and-on fiancée/girlfriend's parents' house, but that option was quashed when the relationship collapsed for the final time. After some nimble string pulling by sympathetic commanding officers, he ended up billeted at Canadian Forces Base Petawawa in an old barracks recently converted into a number of suites, a comfortable little hotel for visiting families and dignitaries. He moved into the single wheelchair-friendly room there.

The building was essentially vacant, but although he was housed alone, he was not left in isolation. There are few places in Canada as close to Afghanistan as CFB Petawawa. Most Canadians receive news of their fallen soldiers in brief radio or television snippets, perhaps a picture in the paper. Of the wounded they hear virtually nothing at all. But Base Petawawa is "The Training Ground of the Warriors." Soldiers who fight in battles live there with their families and friends. It is a place with a deep sense of community, where extended families are vast and loyal. It is a place where no one is afforded the luxury of forgetting their country is at war. There Cpl Dicks was entertained by the troops – treated to a busy convalescence of afternoon outings and backyard summer barbecues. Some days he made his way up a makeshift ramp through a loading bay into the supply shop where he spent his time doing what he could, which was little, but he was welcomed and occupied. There he was with his kind, and all saw he was left no opportunity to languish.

His rehabilitation proceeded. Three or four times each week, he struggled through intense physiotherapy. After some months he was able to lift himself out of the wheelchair and into a walker; some weeks after that he levelled up to a cane. He officially returned to work, logging in half weeks at supply. It was a gift. When his stay in the wheelchair suite ended, he moved back to his apartment, but it was too much too fast. There were too many steps. Up was painful and exhausting. Down was dangerous. He searched out other accommodations and was granted a PMQ (Private Married Quarters), and took on a roommate, a friend from his unit who had been on leave at the time of the explosion.

Life at Petawawa went on. By January he was working full-time on "light" duties. Though he had regained much of his former strength, there were still too many things he was unable to do. He saw men off as he welcomed others back. He watched his mates and colleagues – his fellow soldiers – pass by. He was sidelined, a spectator, unaffiliated. Despite all good intentions and relationships forged, he had been separated from his group and faced a future of constantly being shuffled between units as they came and went. There was no epiphany; it was a gradual understanding that to continue to serve, he knew he too must go.

He requested a posting to Base Borden, one of the largest training bases in the country, where there would be more opportunities. And besides, there was this girl. She went to Georgian College in Orillia. Courtney.

In September he started at Base Borden, hulking behind the front desk at Canadian Forces Support Training Group Imagery, the only position available to him. There he filled out work orders and dispensed completed jobs for an Air Force section made up of photographers and artists. There they were friendly and welcoming. They even let him dabble in their craft. But this was not the army he knew.

His desire was to remain Armour and be redeployed – to go back. But as each day passed, he could see that future falling away, exposing the fear he would one day become inconsequential. He considered teaching. He had the experience; all he lacked were the rank and the qualifications. He would need to pass his PLQs (Primary Leadership Qualifications), but first he would need to prove he was battlefield ready. The BFT (Battlefield Fitness Test) is a thirteen kilometre march with weapon and full kit followed immediately by a one hundred meter fireman's carry, all completed within two hours and twenty minutes. It took him two difficult months to reach a point where he was ready to be tested. On a warm spring morning in 2009, roughly two years to the day after his squad had been torn apart by a land mine halfway around the world, Corporal Matthew Dicks set out.

So picture a man walking. Weighted by the memories of fallen comrades and a trusting friend hoisted onto his shoulders, he steps across a finish line with eleven minutes to spare. His pain is incredible, but he has never felt better. He doesn't yet know he will be unable to complete the physical requirements of his PLQs. He doesn't know he will receive The Sacrifice Medal or that he will be granted the move out from behind the desk at Imagery to in-the-field patrolling the firing ranges. He doesn't yet know he will request to re-muster into a more suitable trade. He doesn't know Courtney will say "Yes" to his proposal and they will be married the following summer. Nor does he know that shortly after the wedding, he will learn he is going to become a father. He is twenty-five years old; he doesn't know his future, what joy and sorrow it will bring. All he knows is that he has one, he is alive, and he is a soldier still.

Strangers to the Boy

"Missing" posters are a common sight where we live. Found most often on mailboxes and hydro poles, and always on the bulletin board outside the variety store at the 5th line, they list species, breed, colour, name, then a last-seen location and date, all ending with a number to call. Their accompanying photographs are pixilated and runny, no doubt favorites peeled from bedroom walls along with little swatches of blue or pink paint. Then you come across one that is different from the rest: one that tugs on your sleeve with its novelty and follows you home with its ubiquity, and no matter how hard you try, you can't seem to shoo it away because it is not of a lost pet at all – it is of a missing boy.

Reclaimed, cleared of tracks and paved over with crushed stone, the Oro-Medonte Rail Trail passes peacefully through its woods and meadows. We walk it Sunday mornings in a ritual with three objectives: to exercise our middle-aged bodies, to sufficiently tire out the dog in order to enjoy a quiet afternoon, and to talk. On the Rail Trail we discuss household matters – work schedules, finances, appointments, meal planning – passively organizing the humdrum while the dog chases whiffs, darting ahead only to linger back, testing both her confidence and our tolerance. Where it intersects roadways, three metal posts protect the trail from prohibited vehicles. On the middle one was where we first saw his face.

The fact that we hadn't heard anything about a missing boy made it immediately obsolete: the over reaction to a child's tantrum, a remnant of premature panic. One in the same place at the next intersection somehow confirmed this and we turned back convinced he was home, warm, safe and, hopefully, grounded. Then there was one at the variety store when we returned our movie rental. Then there was one on the hydro pole at the corner.

On the news that evening his story led. While setting the table we learned his name was Brandon Crisp and he was fifteen years old. On October 13th, after a quarrel with his parents over a video game, he packed a small knapsack and left home on his bicycle. That was a week ago and he was still gone. His bike was discovered abandoned on the Rail Trail near the 3rd line. A witness had said he'd appeared to be struggling with it. The police were making their standard request for tips from anyone who had seen anything no matter how insignificant it may seem. We ate our supper lamenting our world in the hands of this new generation, interrupting our judgments only long enough to catch the weather.

The next week was filled with him. Lines of police in reflective yellow vests marched though ditches and fields with their heads bowed as if in prayer along a zigzagged pilgrimage. We kept track of their progress, reporting to ourselves where we saw them each day, comparing it to where they had been the day before. We took delight in seeing the K9 unit at work. We were surprised when an officer in an ATV popped out from a hidden bush trail. Every day we were stopped and questioned, confronted by his poster again, and every evening his story continued to lead the news, spreading with each repetition, leaping from local to regional to national, even international broadcasts. We found ourselves puzzled by it. We searched for reasons. We invented scenarios. We made up excuses.

The subject of a civilian search planned for the weekend was broached with feigned flippancy, each of us uncertain what distance the other wanted to keep from it all, uncertain of our own willingness to commit. We couldn't say if it was important to us. The announcements warned it was hunting season and volunteers would be required to wear blaze orange clothing. For those without any, there would be plenty of vests on hand, of course. We chose to get our own, cloaking our apprehension in the rationalization that, since there are few streetlights and no sidewalks were we live, we should have some anyway, for walking the dog during dark winter evenings.

The search was based down the road at Burl's Creek Family Event Park. Cars were ushered through wire gates to a grass field. A number of restaurant franchise's event trailers smoked and steamed among a handful of crooked tents. Their attendants shivered over grills and ovens, not yet acclimatized to the cold autumn day, handling everything with long tongs to protect themselves as much from the cold drinks as from the hot food. We milled about awaiting direction. Standing between two metal barrels, a woman was collecting and distributing traffic vests. New volunteers were shown to a school bus idling near the exit at the far end of the lot. Veterans returning were directed to the largest tent, one promising coffee and doughnuts, possibly even cake. A young woman with a note pad hurried about like a mosquito as her accompanying camera team lowered a boom mike into conversations that ended the moment it was discovered. When they began to close in, we made for the bus.

The bus was quiet the way a church is before service. Whispered comments fluttered about, indistinct and irrelevant. Three teenage girls huddled together in a single seat – not the giggling nymphs you see at the mall debating the order in which to enter the store where the cute guy from the other school works. Here they were respectful and solemn. They looked his age and probably went to his school. It was easy to imagine they shared classes with him, they were friends of his. Maybe one of them "liked" him. Maybe one of them had gone out to a show or a party with him, maybe held his hand – perhaps snuck a kiss.

There were others there, too, who would know him. They had seen him before at a school function or sporting event. Their kids had played on the same team or possibly an opposing one. Or maybe not even that close. Maybe their connection to him was more with a parent or sibling, a cousin, a friend of a friend. But if asked if they knew him they would honestly answer "Yes," because a thread of his life was entangled with theirs.

The rest of us were strangers to the boy. A week ago he did not exist; and if not for this, he never would have. Yet we lined up before the woman at the barrels, taking vests out then tossing them in because we have feelings that nudge us, communities that ask of us, religions that require us, and fears that command us. The windows on the bus dripped with the condensation of a million reasons refracting into a single grey blur.

An orange ribbon marked where the last group had ended and we were to begin. Here we were set up like soldiers before filing

21

into a dense bush. Our instructions included maintaining distance and step with our immediate neighbors. The floor tricked with soft mossy ditches and in hard knotted roots. Quick branches whipped necks and faces. Within minutes walking sticks were pulled from the limb debris and distributed to those without. The most useful of tools, they kept us from stumbling through the woods and then let us continue beating our swathe through neck-high meadow grass.

Those in homes we came across were courteous. The cops had already been through the property, they said, but we were welcome to take a second look. They all knew about the boy. A rumour circulated through our team that one property owner denied access to another search party earlier in the day. According to our team captain, if that happened to us, all we could do was inform the police. It wasn't long before we added "grow-op" to the rumour in order to satisfy ourselves.

We were tired, sore, scraped and bruised when we boarded the bus back to base. We had been out for hours and had walked miles through deceitful terrain. We had sweated and chilled. We had fallen and stood waiting for others who had fallen. We had waded through littered ditches and golden meadows. We had weaved through trees, climbed over fallen logs, and disentangled ourselves from raspberry brambles. But we had discovered no signs of the boy.

No one had.

The woman between the barrels was only collecting now. The buses were being swept out. The event vehicles were closing up. In the coffee tent there was still some coffee, a bit of cake and a handful of pizza slices that we passed up on our way back to the car. The search would be continuing tomorrow and we knew we would be back.

The next morning we walked the Rail Trail. The sky hung on the edge of rain, windless and still, silent but for our rhythmic steps and the accompanying drum-roll prancing of the dog as she ran around us in what seemed a desperate attempt to burn off the neglect she'd suffered the day before. Household matters no longer mattered. All was awash in grayscale. Shapes were undefined. The only colour came from little orange ribbons tied in intervals to broken runs of rusted fence and the vests of figures that appeared and then disappeared in our narrow horizon – unofficial volunteers on unofficial trails.

Our pace was slower than usual because we couldn't stop looking, scanning into this rare wilderness. What secrets hung from these trees, huddled behind these boulders, floated in these streams, were covered over by these leaves? Could you run fast enough through the brambles and thickets? Would your cries be heard? Macabre thoughts, those persistent sneaks, hissed with sour breath in our ears. There was only so far into the woods you could see before there was nothing but shadow. Anything could disappear here. Anyone. Reaching the roadway had never before felt so welcome.

That afternoon it rained and we kept moving forward. The coordinators and volunteers at base camp looked tired and in their eyes you could see a disintegrating map as buses radiated further and further from where his bicycle had been found. Our section ended when we reached the lake. We climbed back aboard the bus cold, tired and soaked through. No one complained that the bus just couldn't seem to warm up enough.

In the coffee tent we sipped warmth from paper cups and huddled so close to electric heaters our jackets steamed. Things were being packed up and the announcement was made that the civilian search was being suspended. It would not continue. It was over. No one moved. Hundreds had shown up and hundreds had searched and each one feared being the one to find him and all knew finding nothing was worse. Only the second announcement convinced us to go home.

Every night his story continued to make the news, but the media struggled as each day passed with nothing new to report and it all seemed to be slipping from diminishing priority into increasing surrealism. School officials discussed the problems associated with addressing students' confusion and grief. Parents were shying from quarreling with their teenagers. Video games were vilified and championed. Blame was lobbed about. A reward was anted up and raised. Comparable stories were related. Talk shows worked it. The boy was becoming a symbol. He was teenagers, parenting, sloth, excess, naiveté, indulgence, competition, society. Rumours trickled over bars and tables because there had to be a villain. Candlelight flickered on the faces of congregations singing and praying in vigil because there had to be a God. Police ramped up their efforts because hope lingered. We continued to be stopped and asked the same serious questions in an attempt to jog our memories of anything … anything at all.

Autumn stayed on schedule. One day it snowed, but not enough to last – not yet. As its kaleidoscope of ripened colours tumbled to earth and dissolved into grey, we explored areas of the Rail Trail we hadn't before – watching the dog, letting her wander further and further from us, investigating everything that caught her interest. Some days we took different routes home. We couldn't stop searching.

On November 5th a group of hunters discovered a body fitting the boy's description. Any official pronouncement would not be made until it was proven to be his, but we knew it was. He'd been right there all along. North of Ridge Road between the 4th and 5th lines, about two kilometers from where he'd abandoned his bicycle, a boy we'd never met had fallen from a tree and died.

We had missed him.

We still miss him.

GEORGE BELAJAC

GEORGE is a retired school teacher living in Orillia, Ontario with his wife, Elizabeth. His inspirations often stem from personal experiences. George's children, grandchildren and former students frequently become the focal point of his writing. He strives to blend interesting characters and story telling in his poetry and short stories. George continues to pursue and enjoy his avid enthusiasm in sports. After many years of coaching and participating, he now assumes an armchair delivery.

As an ongoing member of The Mariposa Writers' Group, George has shared in the annual Lake Country Literary Lapses Festival Poetry and Short Story Competitions, as well as participating in the various events held by the Festival. George's enthusiasm for writing has resulted in his poetry being published in anthologies such as *A Golden Morning, Shadow of the Dawn* and *Island Skies*. He is presently completing his final edit of a juvenile novel.

Tsunami

Ivory castles glisten in the sun
As nature unleashes giants
Undetected - surging
Swirling currents in every direction
Heads surface - gasping for survival
Faces of sorrow
Faces of bewildered innocence
Destruction beyond imagination
Tragedy untold
Shadows of death saturate the ruins
The castles undefiled
A time to honour life!
To descend the steps
For existence is a privilege
One child looks into another's eyes
They read but cannot speak
Tears swell the heart
Hands reach out
A line in the sand
Horror – despair
Relentless suffering
Searching for compassion – to calm
The world awakens
To celebrate humanity for all time
O' fear not hope!
For existence is a privilege
Happiness a duty

Dear Gramma and Grampa

You ask, what can you leave me when you are gone?
I seek not your riches or fame
I am but a child of my mother's womb
And just been given a name
But please leave the knowledge to shape and mould
And the tools to start right away
My earth is being wasted so quickly now
There cannot be further delay
Will I see forests that reach the sky
And taste water so cool and clean
Will you leave the oceans full of life
With wonders never seen
Will I hear the sound of a meadow lark
Or a babbling brook in the glen
Will the birds and animals be safe and free
Protected by all men
Will I see the sun, the moon and stars
And their beauty in full surrender
Will the day and night be our guiding lights
Forever their magic to render
Will I feel the wind and see the clouds
Will the snowflakes touch my face
Will the sun's precious rays bring harvest aplenty
For the entire human race
And will the air I breathe be fresh each day
And bring life to all that surrounds me
Will it be the same for all people on earth
Because this is how it should be!
Please Gramma and Grampa promise to try and do your best
If you really love ME so
Will you tell all your friends in the whole wide world
So that they too will know

The Chesterfield

It was grubby but comfortable
Two pillows and a blue throw furbished it
I could dive into it from three feet away
And be out like a light in seconds
Burying my thoughts into deep and tranquil solitude
I could do anything I wanted
I could be anyone I wanted
I could take a piece of magic from a storybook
And instantaneously be in its midst
I might even be in some sort of partnership
With Hercules or be an acquaintance of Juno's
If I faked right I could zoom down the opposite sideline
To instant glory
I might even drive dad's Chevy Malibu V-8
To the Friday night dance at the "Kee"
Nothing but honesty
If I wanted a playback of the day
I'd keep my eyes open
Then I'd think through – whatever......
I could even dream
And often,
She would be on my mind
I was smitten from the moment I saw her
Her brown purse and brown high heels
Complimented her tan suede coat with its fur collar
She had a perfect walk
Her looks left my head spinning
Her tender glance heightened my deepest desire
It was time to meet her
And the honesty of that fact
Caused me to sink deeper
Into the comfort of the chesterfield
And hug my pillow even tighter
Somehow I knew - that I would come to love her

Summer Storm

Zorro's mark dances in ecstasy
Flashing in the veil of the sweltering heat
The Jedi Masters wield their light sabres
Deftly challenging
Shrewdly avoiding the surging giants
Dressed in battle fatigue - emblazoned in coal black
Angered - ready to charge
Echoes in the distant horizon - an ominous warning
Drums of an ancient tribe
The warriors strain to pierce the silence
Thor nods
The fiery light explodes like a million candles
Unmasking the darkness
Eerie silhouettes - black and white pictures
Vibrations - a frame shatters on the floor
As nature unleashes

Grandpa's Secret Plan

My red wagon was faded and blistered by the sun. Its wheel covers were dinted and its black rubber tires worn so flat in spots that it wobbled and bumped on flat ground. And even though the wooden handle was chipped and bent, my hand fit around it perfectly. Other kids had wagons but mine looked more like a work wagon than a fun and racing one.

Grandpa brought it to our house one day when I was five. He told me he got it for free from a friend, "You've always got hand-me-downs 'cause you're the youngest, so …ah…here's another, I guess. I didn't have time to fix it up or do anything special to it, but I thought you might like something of your own." I gave him a big hug and just took it as it was. "Thanks, Grandpa, you're the best!"

I was embarrassed by its appearance. Some kids had new oak wagons all varnished, with spoke wheels and even words painted on the sides. These kids smirked at my work wagon. So for a year I didn't overuse it. But when I turned six, my little red wagon began to fill my heart with pride.

On my birthday, Grandpa came for a visit and told me about a secret plan. I was not to tell anyone. It was our secret! Grandpa explained that I could use the little red wagon to load some defective aircraft parts that were dumped at the back of Buchanan Engines daily. Every third day most of the parts were loaded on a truck and hauled away. Now Grandpa had spotted copper and brass fittings scattered in the pile and he decided to talk to Bob at the local scrap yard. Bob agreed that if I brought him wagonloads of these fittings he'd pay a reasonable amount for them.

Wouldn't you know it? Grandpa supervised my first load to Bob's scrap yard! So when I arrived home and presented my mom with a whole dollar bill, she asked where I got it. Grandpa let me tell the whole story. Mom, with tears in her eyes squashed me in a big hug to her flowered apron. My dad and brothers patted me on the back and praised me about how grown up I was. Grandpa nodded his head and said, "He's a very good boy!"

The brass and copper nuts, bolts and couplings were covered in a grimy oil that made my clothes dirty. On hot days my face was smeared with black streaks where my hands had rubbed away beads of perspiration. I had a bath as soon as I got home. My clothes smelled of javex but that didn't matter. I had a summer job! And soon Grandpa talked Bob into taking two loads a week.

When I trundled my little red wagon twice a week, I felt like a real business man. Bob said, "Thanks young man. You've got some good pieces here!" Sometimes I had to pull with both hands to get up the ridge just before the scrap yard. This was when I had really big loads!

One day something was very different. There was no pile of rejects behind Buchanan's factory. Instead there were just a few rejects that barely covered the bottom of my wagon. Huh, maybe a few cents worth, I thought to myself! I felt embarrassed when I went through the gate into Bob's scrap yard and parked my wagon on the weigh scale. "One whole dollar," said Bob watching the scale hand. "As usual."

For two years Bob did this many times. I never questioned him. Mom used the money to buy clothes and food for our struggling immigrant family. There was always a little bit left over, so I could go to the Saturday matinee with my friends. And each Christmas Bob sent a gift package to our home. It took awhile before I began to understand.

When I was eight, Grandpa died. At the end of my final summer delivery to Bob's scrap yard, I asked my dad to help me put four new wheels on the little red wagon. I gave it a sanding and a fresh coat of paint. The next day I pulled my wagon next door to our neighbours.

Michael was playing on the front steps. He was six. I'm sure my Grandpa smiled down from heaven when he saw me present Michael with my little red wagon.

JIM BUTLER

JIM was born in Montreal and is married to Elspeth Jewett. They have one daughter, Susan Elspeth. He graduated Concordia (B.Sc.) and spent several subsequent years in the Faculty of Commerce.

Jim served in several capacities with the Real Estate Institute of Canada, The Institute of Real Estate Management (Chicago), Montreal Building Owners and Managers Society and subsequently with Toronto BOMA.

Jim joined the Marathon Realty Company at Montreal in February, 1974 and was moved to Toronto in a corporate re-organization in 1981. Following a career in Property Management operations, Jim developed a separate functional national group specializing in Asset and Buildings Technology. He retired in 1993 and settled with his wife in Bayshore Village near Orillia. The Butlers developed an interest in dogs, primarily Doberman Pinschers. They were active in canine conformation and obedience shows.

Jim authored several technical manuals and various trade related and technical papers prepared for a variety of professional organizations. Jim has also been a speaker at various business, building and real estate conferences in Canada.

Moon Landing

Our family lived in Longueuil, on the mainland south shore across from Montreal Island, in July of 1969. Wife Elspeth's brother and family were at that time in Markham, north east of Toronto, in a quite respectable neighbourhood. At that time family birthday celebrations brought us to her brother's house for a few days. As it happened Elspeth, daughter Susan and myself were invited with brother Edwin and his wife Cathy to a barbeque and potluck supper at the home of one of his neighbours. This turned out to be quite a celebration, as the guest list had expanded to include most of the neighbours on that street.

Television in those days was black-and-white; a set had been installed in the back yard and the assembled birthday celebrants kept an eye on the American coverage. Meanwhile, between the very generous quantity of food and the open bar (also potluck) the party continued.

The date was Saturday, July 20th. It was known that the American spaceship Apollo 11, which had launched on July 16 from the Kennedy Space Center in Florida, was expected to arrive at its lunar destination that afternoon. As the scheduled hour approached the crowd's attention was focused on television and the momentous history-making activity occurring above.

At that time Sue, a teen-ager, as usual, was being helpful in the background. At some point she had taken over bartending duties and was busy pouring and delivering drinks to all of the guests. She was, however, apparently pouring the drinks as she infrequently did for me at home – really quite generous ones.

My brother-in-law's neighbours were quite respectable citizens, and it soon became obvious that many in the assembly did not normally over-indulge. The party got loud – quite loud. Fortunately, no one called the constabulary – probably because everyone was in attendance and not inclined to call. However, as the afternoon progressed, neighbours were to be seen staggering up and down the street arm-in-arm and singing, quite loudly, songs that would not have been heard in church.

We did, of course, close the bar – much to the dismay of many of the assembled guests. Fortunately nobody was driving, and some exercise was needed to get back to his or her bed and sleep it off. Messers Armstrong, Collins and Aldrin managed to get the job done without the assistance of the assembly and the landing was a huge success.

It was noted, however, that there were a number of sheep-ish faces around the neighbourhood the following morning.

Time of Use Hydro Rates

Note: Utility companies, including Ontario Hydro, are currently struggling with commercial and domestic peak demand for electrical energy, which is growing at an accelerating pace. Peak demand control has become a norm for the industry; it has also become an economic necessity given the technology of today.

For the purposes of this essay it will be useful to provide several simple definitions:

Watt (W) A unit of electrical energy. Watts are calculated by multiplying electric current (or Amperes) by electrical potential (or Volts). A sixty-watt light bulb would be 0.5 amps x 120 volts.

Kilowatt (kW) this term refers to a measure of DEMAND – means 1,000 watts. For example a current of 8.33 amps at 120 volts (or 8 1/3 x 100 watt incandescent light bulbs. Demand measures the volume of electrical energy being used at a point in time.

Kilowatt hour (kWh) is a measure of CONSUMPTION – refers to the number of kilowatts of energy used in one hour. For example, the 8 1/3 x 100 watt incandescent light bulb turned on for one hour would use 1 kWh of electrical energy.

Time of Use Rates (TOU) The introduction of a TOU or Time-Of use rate structure was developed to encourage property users to retrofit, or to introduce in the design of new properties, systems to control energy demand. Electrical demand in an office building will be much higher during business hours when the building is fully occupied than at midnight when most of the lighting will be shut off, the elevators are parked, the environmental systems are shut down or sharply set back, etc.

Note: Although we refer to the use of electricity as consumption, the term is not strictly accurate. Conventional Physics tells us that energy can be neither created nor destroyed – but it CAN be converted to another form of energy. In the case of an incandescent light bulb, the electrical energy is converted to heat – the heat required to make the element in the light bulb white-hot. This heat is then radiated from the bulb and adds to the temperature of the room, which explains the problems we experience trying to control the temperature of rooms liberally supplied with incandescent pot-

"The International Energy Agency estimates that between now and 2030, global investment electrical grid infrastructure of around $6 trillion will be needed to satisfy the world's increasing demand for power. Most of the growth is expected in Asia with the construction of new transmission and distribution systems, but new investments will also be needed in the United States and Europe where aging systems must be replaced. "

"Meeting the rise in global demand of electricity will mean adding a 1 GW power plant and all related infrastructure every week for the next 20 years." *Ontario Hydro Web Site*"

Supplying electricity at peak times (those times when we're all using a lot of electricity) has several economic impacts.

Why does it matter so much?

- It adds to our electricity costs because higher demand often means higher market prices.

- It's had on the environment because <u>more</u> of the less attractive forms of generation must be used to satisfy user demand.

- It adds to the funds that Ontario Hydro must invest in the system because meeting the demand peaks means building more new generating facilities and more transmission and distribution infrastructure – which also adds to electricity costs.

So working together to reduce peak demand makes sense.

A review of power usage established patterns over the 24-hour day, which varied through the seasons. Commercial buildings require major power availability to control environmental systems. In Summer cooling is needed to offset the heat-load due to occupant heat emission (normal body temperature is 98.6 degrees F. but room temperature is targeted at 72 degrees), waste heat is released by the operation of tools and equipment, solar heat absorbed by windows and by the building 'skin' (glass, metals such as stainless steel or aluminum and/or masonry). Such heat loads are developed during working hours in the winter as well, to the extent that air-conditioning is a year-round requirement in modern office towers – particularly in modern buildings with sealed windows.

Naturally, the heat absorbed by the building load is considerably greater during the summer months when the solar load is much greater. Much of the electricity used in a commercial building is a constant, which is fairly low during the night. Around 7 am on a normal business day, office floor lighting (which, hopefully, has been turned off all night) will be turned on – and lighting can account for 35% to 40% of the total electrical load in a building. The elevators begin their fairly constant daytime operation. The very large ventilation blowers start up, pumps start pumping, and tenant staffs turn on coffee makers, computers, laser printers, photocopiers, etc. These year-around activities can account for up to 65% to 70% of the total energy use – the building chillers can represent the remaining 30% to 35%. If the peak electrical load is 2,000 kW, the chillers can represent up to 600kW or 700 kW. If the Utility is charging $10. per kW demand, this load can represent $6,000 or $7,000 per month.

Analysis of the power used in these buildings will vary considerably over weekends compared to weekdays as well as over the twenty-four hour day. Such change is clearly attributable to office lighting but to an even greater degree to the operation of very large 'chillers' used to control environmental conditions. Balancing of the cooling load in the building must consider:

- Indoor population density on each floor
- Concentration of machinery and equipment
- Fenestration (Windows)
- Solar exposure (Sun load variation through the day)

Other factors:
- Window exposure (mid-floor vs. perimeter location)
- Ventilation control (Air flow volume)
- Chiller size
- Thermal Storage (Mass – Water – Ice)

An important system of demand control would be to provide incentives for both domestic and commercial users to control the use of power. Ontario Hydro identified this idea in the commercial market late in the twentieth century and established programs to encourage usage control at that time. Financial incentives then offered included the establishment of grant programs to support upgrades of systems to improve the efficiency of operation, such as:

- Window film or other insulation of windows
- Sophisticated ventilation control such as computerized systems
- Isolated perimeter systems coordinated with solar load factors
- Variable Air Volume duct diffusers to enable computerized monitoring and control of supply air to interior and perimeter zones
- Computerized lighting systems (turn the lights off!)

Environmental systems in older buildings tended to be "one size fits all" – the design sized the chillers and heating systems to satisfy the expected total demand of the planned occupancy of the building; the theory was opening a window could then provide variation within the space. This approach became impractical as energy costs increased, and systems had to be designed to satisfy local demand in a more practical manner.

Vintage building design tended to use very large chillers – often a single chiller sized to handle the anticipated total demand – which then had to be operated to satisfy even very small loads – (e.g. ground floor retail tenants in major office buildings). Modern practice would be to specify several small systems that could be started individually or sequentially to satisfy demand. It then also became desirable to replace such very large machines by retrofitting in accordance with current standards.

Initially perimeter zones were established, with provision for solar variance (east, west, south and north exposure) by sizing heat and cool supply equipment. Windows incorporated insulation provisions, such as twin glazing, solar screening and other methods. Computerized control of treated water or air distribution systems allowed building operators to direct cooling to satisfy the need.

It was necessary to control floor interior zones as well, and variable air volume supply boxes were designed to be installed on the supply ductwork; a computer program used temperature readings and set-points on each box to controlled these units as needed to maintain the required airflow. These replaced earlier large 'fan-coil' units in which large fans forced constant volumes of air over 'coils' or radiators.

Thermal Storage is an energy conservation tool. Although the term can also refer to the storage of heat, these systems are used in large commercial buildings to control demand by storing cooling capacity (the removal of heat) during off-peak hours by operating the chillers to chill water or make ice.

There are many variations and most utilities have a series of rate schedules tailored to customer size. The monthly bill from the electric utility will always contain a charge for 'consumption' or the total kWh usage, and a charge for demand. For all practical purposes, electricity must be used as it is generated; it can be stored in batteries, but not in very large quantities. Consequently the Utility must have the capacity to generate all the energy all users will need at peak period – whether it is actually used or not. The Utility charges each user proportionately for contributing to this demand capacity, and the charge to each user for the billing period (usually about a month) is based on the peak load (for as short a time as fifteen minutes) during the billing period. This is also the reason for TOU (Time of Use) rates – if some of the load can be transferred to an "off-peak" period (particularly after midnight) when the electricity can be generated without needing to add to the generating equipment.

There are two types of thermal storage systems available to control cooling demand.

- Stratified Chilled Water Storage works like an electric battery except that instead of electrical energy the system stores large volumes of water which can be chilled through the night to temperatures in the range of 42 deg.F to 45 deg.F. This water can then be used to remove heat from the building during the following day. The tanks used to store this water are very large – capacities can range to one-half million gallons. In this system water is taken from the base of the tank, passed through the building to absorb waste heat and returned to the top of the tank. Water is taken from the top of the tank by a different system, passed through the cooling process in the chiller and returned to the base. Provided the flow is controlled to avoid physical disturbance that would initiate convective heat transfer, a THERMOCLINE or separation of the dense chilled water and the less dense warm water will allow controlled discharge of the tank over a period of days.

- Ice Storage is does not require the space needed for the very large water tank, but does require specially designed chillers capable of reducing the temperature of Glycol to 28 deg.F. These units can make ice (with in a heat exchanger) during the low-demand hours – the ice is then used to cool the building during business hours.

Thermal storage systems (water or ice) can be sized to provide complete redundancy (use of chillers ONLY during the TOU time window) or to reduce the chiller load during peak load time periods and transfer this load to other parts of the day. This may include evening hours when some cooling is still required to satisfy office tenants working overtime and to accommodate retail tenants; if the chiller must be operated, the system can be set at an efficient level and the surplus capacity used to chill water in the tank or to make ice.

The decision on design capacity is an economic one. Addition of a thermal storage system to a building adds considerable dollars to the cost, and this additional investment must be recovered. The recovery will be based on reduced energy cost.

The decision to include thermal storage in new buildings can be supported economically by the reduced cost of energy in operations provided by TOU factors (and the payback for this investment can be quite short) and well as by the reduction of sizing in selection of the chillers. These systems also contribute substantially to energy conservation and consequently reduce environmental concerns through reduced burning of fossil fuels (which produce Carbon Dioxide – a contributor to global warming, etc.) or through reduction of the need for additional nuclear facilities. The building owner/developer, therefore, makes a contribution to the environment.

Because of the area required to accommodate a water-based thermal storage tank, they are not practical for use in a retrofit situation. It is, however, feasible to use ice storage in such situations, and this possibility should always be considered closely when chiller replacement or supplementation is being considered.

DOREEN CALDWELL

DOREEN was born September 28, 1930. She is the daughter of Charlie and Ida Thornton. Her dad was a well known auctioneer in Central Ontario.

Doreen went to Murdock's Business College from 1946 to 47. She worked at the Oro Station Switchboard from 1950 to 57 and also farmed in Shanty Bay.

Doreen married Murray Caldwell on September 20, 1952 and had two children, Dwight who was born June 14, 1957 and Gina who was born August 3, 1961.

Murray, Moose and Me

If you want to accompany your husband on a hunting trip, make sure he wants you along. Don't nag him into taking you; but if you are invited to go, then do it!

I was my husband Murray's companion on four moose hunting trips to Northern Ontario where we had many adventures. As a new mom with a 3-month old the first challenge I faced was finding a babysitter for our son Dwight. Fortunately my Mother Ida Thornton took on the task and I was free to go.

On our first trip in 1959 we towed our hardtop trailer to Silverwater first, to camp and fish. Next we travelled to Hearst were we met our pilot Percy Bradley and left our car at his beautiful house. Percy flew Murray and I, and our companions Ron and Graydon, in his bush plane, deep into the woods to Tower Lake, and despite the weather and heavy load, we weren't too scared.

When we arrived, Murray and I put up our tent and the two men took the cabin. They seemed to think I was there to cook and do their dishes, but I stood my ground and told them "no way. I'm here to hunt, too" and that was that. While we were setting up, they spotted a moose and asked Murray to help them track and shoot it; but we were tired and Murray wanted to sleep, so we left them to it and they came back empty handed.

On our first day of hunting Murray ran ahead of me into the bush and I was left alone. I was upset but I knew it was a test and he would come back for me, and he did. Although we went out every day, we didn't get a moose but it was a great learning experience for me. That year we returned "mooseless" to Orillia but I was able to use what I learned to stay warm, comfortable and safe on our future trips. Here are some things to remember when planning your hunt with your husband.

Warm clothes are vital if you want to enjoy yourself. I felt snug in two pairs of heavy socks and fur lined moccasins that I stuck into rubber boots. I also took two sweaters, a quilted jacket and woollen kerchief for my head, as well as warm mittens. You should also plan to take a pair of waterproof mittens along if part of the trip is to done by canoe. When you paddle, your woollen mittens get wet. You can be very unhappy with freezing hands. Also it's best to wear something orange or yellow so no one will mistake you for a moose! Take some reading material along too, for those rainy days and long nights in the tent.

And don't forget your gun! I carried a double barrelled shotgun. I am never afraid in the bush as long as I have either my husband or my gun with me. I can handle the gun and would use it if I had to; but on one trip my husband and the guide went up river for about 25 minutes and I grew nervous and frightened because I didn't have my gun. I didn't let that happen again!

Sadly after flying us out in 1959, Percy Bradley was later killed in an airplane crash and we no longer flew to our hunting area.

In 1960 we went to Wawa. We travelled by car with a canoe tied to the top of the Volkswagen. Murray and I carried all of our gear deep into the bush and set up our tent by ourselves, but we did not get a shot and back to Orillia we went, still without our moose. Oh well, we did get away from it all. Maybe next year we would be luckier and to help out we decided to hire an Indian guide.

In 1961 we went to the Kabina River area. We had an Indian guide named, Mos Pete. All of our equipment, including a Coleman stove and lamps, the tent, sleeping bags, quilts; our food (instant potatoes, milk powder and believe it or not, jars of baby food) was packed into three sacks and we carried it 28 miles through the bush to our camp. Each day we covered many miles of bush country on foot and by canoe along the river, without seeing a moose. The weather was not as cold as it could have been, but it rained every day. Black flies, normally absent in the colder season, were quite a nuisance, despite protective sprays. Then on the last day, my husband Murray was walking on a road near our camp when a moose stepped right out in front of him. But he had no gun and the moose left unharmed. I was in the tent and missed it all. So once again it was home empty handed.

We returned to the same location in 1962. By now I knew that hunting for moose required lots of patience and good luck. Rise and shine time was 7:30 a.m. and one morning after breakfast was prepared I called for the men. Mos Pete had already gone alone into the bush and a little later Murray had set out down the dirt road to meet him. I heard shots and went running. I found them standing beside a big bull moose lying dead on the road. Mos said the moose had stepped right out in front of him, but he and Murray both claimed to have shot it. Men! I didn't care. We had finally bagged our moose! Mos had already bled the carcass and we combined forces to dress it. Mos and I held the moose and Murray cut it up into quarters with a hunting knife and we put the pieces into sugar bags. We took the back seat out of the car and packed the bags of meat in there and tied the horns to the top of the car. With no refrigeration available we had to start for home right away. We took turns taking pictures of each other, standing by the car, pointing to the moose horns on the roof. We did stop on the way to report our kill to the MNR and get a success crest.

Once back in Orillia, we went to the butcher and the meat was cut into serving portions and stored in the freezer locker. We ended up with about 500 pounds of boneless meat for our four day trip, at a cost of about $300, which included a hunting license, and expenses. That year we saved about $200 on the winter's meat bill.

We did however have one problem. The blood from the meat we packed into the back seeped through the bags on to the floor of our car and we were forced to trade it in! We hope the dealer cleaned it up for the new owner.

We mounted the moose antlers in our home and each year after that I decorated them with ribbons and bows at Christmas. They were a lasting reminder of the trials, fun and success of Murray and me and the bagging of that unfortunate moose.

The Thornton Chronicles
"The Great Auctioneer's Daughter"

The saga of the Thorntons begins with the courtship and marriage of my parents, Ida McKee and Charles H. Thornton.

My mother, Ida was born in May 1902, one of the ten children of John McKee and Catherine (Meher) McKee. She and her siblings, Liz, Jim, Murdock, Nellie, Emma, Flossie, Minnie (who died), Laurene and Olive went to school at Uhthoff and Northbrook. Mr. Robins was the school teacher. He was very strict, but he had to be for the older boys. Ida was a good student and did well in "spelling bees" usually winning first place. She completed grade seven and her dream was to be a registered nurse. But there was no money, so to help out the family she went to work early doing housework for rich people. My father, Charles, was also a member of a large family. He was the son of Sam and Katherine Thornton and he and his nine brothers and sisters lived in a two bedroom log home in Carolyn and they attended the Carolyn school. They were a poor family and to save wear, the kids took their shoes off after the snow had melted and walked to school barefoot. As a young boy Charlie visited auction sales with his family and became fascinated with the speed and skill of the auctioneers. He started practicing to be an auctioneer when he was in grade two and he would show off his skill for the people at some of the sales. God gave him a talent and he used it.

Everyone wanted to see what Charlie could do and he often went to the Farmers' Market at the Opera House in Orillia and auctioned wood, cattle, horses and other stock. At the age of 16 he also started to "call" square dances. He spent three years "calling" in the logging camps and was so popular he travelled all over Simcoe County, Mara and Rama Townships.

One special night he came down to the Hall on the 5th Concession, to call a square dance and met Ida McKee. His friend Bill Elliott told him to "make a date" with Ida because she was a wonderful housekeeper and dancer. His rival Archie Lahay wanted to date Ida too and Charlie didn't think she would dance with him; but when he asked her, he was happy and surprised when she said "yes" right away.

Ida and Charles went together for three years. They picnicked together at Uhthoff and they danced all the time, even when he was calling the dances. When in Uhthoff, Ida would take her handicapped sister Flossie too and Charlie was kind to her and they became good friends for life. When apart, Ida and Charlie wrote romantic letters to each other to stay in touch.

In June of 1926, Charles asked Ida to become engaged, His exact words were "Do you have any objections to being my wife?" She said "no" and a date was set.

The wedding was held at the McKee homestead. They were married by Reverend Mason and Earn Thornton was best man for Charles. Her sister, Flossie McKee was bridesmaid for Ida and nieces, nine-year old Dot Langman and Elsie Wainman were the flower girls.

Catherine McKee was the hostess and she invited all of the in-laws, sisters and husbands and brothers and wives and their kids and all by herself organized a buffet lunch for 65.

Later that day they had a community dance and shower with 250 guests at Uhthoff Hall and the party lasted until four in the morning. Angus Duncan and Charlie took turns calling the dances so Charlie and Ida could dance together.

The newlyweds took a honeymoon trip by train to Alliston to visit Ida's sister Emma and her husband Jesse. They couldn't leave their farm and children to come to the wedding so Charlie and Ida went to them. They stayed four days and with Emma's ten kids running around it was not very quiet or private. Some "honeymoon"!

They returned to set up house in Charlie's two bedroom log home in Carolyn. They started farming staked by the $60.00 in Ida's bank account and Charlie's notes on cattle, horses and furniture.

Tom Smith was their hired man for 14 years. He slept in one bedroom and Ida and Charlie slept in the other. Tom and Charlie did the heavy farm work and Ida did some of the chores and kept the log house. They had eight cows that Charlie bought at sales and Ida, who was a wonderful milker, cared for them.

I was born on September 28, 1930. Grandma asked Mum to name me after her and she did and that's how I got my name. Amelia Doreen Thornton. I have also have a nickname, "Dorie" as Dad called me; but Mum always insisted on calling me Doreen because that was what she named me and she called me so until the day she died. My brother Ivan was born November 30, 1934 at the log house. It was very cold and Mum had a hard birth which affected her health later in life.

We lived in the log house from 1928 to 1937 and my best gift as a child was a lamb that Dad gave to me. During the "Great Depression" we had a tough time and had to have a sale because we were broke. Dad had to auction the sale of his own possessions. It must have been hard for him. There were 250 people there and he did very well. Bill Calverley was so impressed he took Dad to see Mr. Warner on 6th Concession, for a sale. Dad had to admit that he didn't have a license or the money to buy one, but Mr. Warner told him not to worry and paid the $10.00 fee. Dad had his first official sale and would go on to conduct over 3000 sales during the next 47 years.

Ivan usually stayed with Mum to help at the farm and I travelled with Dad and even went to Council meetings with him. Sometime Ivan and I were both let off school to go to sales. But I still did my share of the chores in the barn and with machine work.

During that time Dad spent most of his time auctioneering and calling dances. Until he could afford a car, Bill Calverley drove him to the sales and the name Charlie Thornton "Auctioneer" went right to the top in the auction sales trade.

In fact a noted writer about auctions, Mr. Joyelle Shani was so impressed he wrote about Dad in a special "trade" Newsletter. Here are some quotes:

"Recognized leader in auctioneering Charles H. Thornton has marked ability for conducting auction sales. In a review of the business interests of this section there is no one more worthy of mention than Charles H. Thornton.

His ability as an auctioneer stands second to none in this part of the country. His wide and comprehensive experience together with his inherent ability have made him a recognized leader in this profession. He knows values and deals equally fair with his employer and the public.

A pleasant personality, a jovial disposition and a keen insight of human nature win for him sales and friends at the same time. If you would have your sales conducted right, secure the services of Charles H. Thornton. You may depend upon his integrity as a man and as an auctioneer. His sales are conducted in a snappy manner. without waste or loss of time.

The community is indeed fortunate in having a man of such rare and efficient ability. We wish to congratulate him on his success."

When Dad read the article he was the proudest and happiest man you ever did see and I still have and treasure that clipping.

Dwight and I hosted a 50th Anniversary celebration for Mum and Dad at Guthrie Hall on June 20, 1978. Dad had suffered a stroke in March of 1976 and he had to try his hardest to dance. But with Mum's help he was able to do it. He was proud and happy to be able to dance with his beautiful bride 50 years after their wedding day. I did the announcing for the large crowd in attendance and I think I did a great job. Ivan my brother wished them health and happiness and many more years of life as husband and wife. Dad died November 23, 1984 of a stroke and Mum died October 27, 1998. Ivan died three weeks later on November 24.

Now, only I am left to tell the story of Charlie and Ida Thornton, and no one could be prouder than I to be known as the daughter of "the great auctioneer" Charlie Thornton.

FRANK DAULBY

FRANK was born in Winnipeg, Manitoba. He is a retired police officer specializing in Forensics, Statement Analysis and Composite Art.

Frank took up short story fiction writing in 2009.

Frank won first place in Lake Country Literary Lapses' Short Story Contest 2009 and 2010.

Jean and Arlo
Winner of the Lake Country Literary Lapses' Festival
Short Fiction Competition

Jean was a nasal toned, tattooed squib of a girl. A mother's love. All arms and legs, vile things that betrayed her confidence. She wore close-cut yellow hair tucked behind her ears, a pair of blue-rimmed glasses and red running shoes.

She rolled the garbage bag over the dumpster's edge. "The Grill's" back alley exhaust fan droned overhead. Its pungent odour stuck to the sole of New York City like chewing gum. She took a drag from her cigarette, tossed her head back and spit her gum in a high arch. She squatted, pulled her white apron taut over her knees and rolled back into a nest of cupped produce boxes to stare into a fierce blue New York sky. A quick thrum of raindrops blossomed around her; castoffs from the skyscrapers towering above her.

The alleyway was Jean's refuge.

O-bi-jou, played on her iPod as Arlo rode into the alley on a stolen bicycle. He dumped it on the ground and walked over to her.

--Bum a smoke?

She ignored him.

--Bum a smoke?

--Get lost.

Arlo stepped back and bent over to look her in the eye.

--What?

--What. She stared back. His scuffed size twelve, second-hand brogue shoes an awkward reality; out of sync with the lyrics dancing in her head. She tugged out one ear-bud and squinted up at his silhouette.

--What?

--Can I bum a smoke?

Her gaze settled on his knees, at the holes fashioned in his pants . . . very original.

--Come on. One won't kill you.

--Who the-frig are you?

--A guy needing a smoke, come on?

--You got fifty cents?

--You got allergies?

--You want a smoke, or not?

--This your last one? Arlo wedged the offered cigarette behind his ear, pulled open the restaurant's service door and walked through the garden of boxed carrots and cabbage into the rear of the diner. Jean sat stunned. . . jumped up and yelled "frigger." She flicked her cigarette off the brick wall . . . stomped over to the door, paused, turned back and kicked out the spokes of his bicycle.

She took a deep breath, tied up her hair and strolled back into The Grill. She spotted Arlo seated in the end booth. She took a few table orders, pulled two waiting breakfast specials from under the heat lamps, walked over and gave his booth a kick.

--Gimme my smokes.

--One smoke, he replied.

--Gimme my cigarette.

--You first. Gimme a menu.

Jean paused, backed up, set down the two orders and grabbed her cigarette from behind his ear. She spun around, bit her lip and pulled her apron string out of his hand and headed back to the pickup window.

--That him? "White Buck," the cook asked.

Jean ignored him.

--That him?

--Who?

--Him . . . you know.

--For frig sakes, who?

--Our new short-order cook.

--No. Some . . . . She fought the urge to say 'A-hole'.

--Some A-hole. She broke a surprised giggle.

--Well the A-hole is eating your double order, Buck snickered.

--Jeese. Jean hissed, stomped over and grabbed the plates.

--No.

--Too slow. Arlo grinned. He pulled one plate back.

--You're paying for that.

Something was up. He was too cheeky to be a real customer. She retreated to the pick-up counter. She set the remaining order under a heat lamp, leaned in and watched Buck, a Métis from Saskatoon, Saskatchewan portion out a fresh order. He was a luncheon plate taller than she with a round pock marked face sewn under a full head of shiny black hair. A pony tail rode his shoulders when he pulled off his hair net. He drew an *X* next to her *0* on the stainless steel counter in their ongoing Tic-tac-toe game.

--You think that's who Kevin hired? he asked.

--No. . . . You recognize him?

--No, but he seems to know you.

--He took my cigarette, is all . . . Kevin in today?

--Don't know.

--Did he leave our cheques?

--Don't know.

--Thanks, Buck.

She leaned over the counter and grabbed a bit of bacon off a plate, toyed with it, tossed it in the garbage and stared into tomorrow. . . . Her grandmother would be sleeping perhaps forgetting her. Her volunteer care worker would be watching television.

--Hey, 'white biscuit' it's your move.

Jean looked down at the tic-tac-toe game and drew a *0* in a square with the wax pencil. A sudden boom shook the diner. She grabbed the counter but her spindly legs folded under her. She dropped to her knees. Wine bottles toppled. Plaster fell. The air conditioner faltered. The diner went black. Patrons gasped. An endless moment hung in silence. The emergency lights came on.

Earthquake. sang a chorus of believers.

The front door burst open. Placemats cycloned up past talking mouths. Tables twisted off matchbook-balanced legs.

--Shut the door. Arlo shouted, shouldering his way over to watch a deluge of sidewalk-sale clothing in a havoc of tables and chairs. All catapulted down the street. A dozen people jumped up, tossed cash onto the counter. They were thrashing into a knot at the front door when the second boom shifted the tiny diner.

--What's happening? a woman yelled.

--Close the door. Arlo shouted.

--Two planes. Someone yelled.

--Two planes hit the twin towers.

Within seconds, The Grill, was filled with uncomprehending stares. People on cell-phones, anxious hands with car and house keys, at the ready. Jean slammed the twisted door shut and flipped the *closed sign*. Several more people were let in. Many were let out before Jean's panicked voice yelled.

--No more. That's enough.

Screaming now.

--That's enough.

She tried to lock the door, gave up and ran to the rear of the diner. She needed to leave. She stopped and stared at the payphone. Her eighty year old, grandmother . . . now a worry but far removed, safe, cared for, in their sublevel bachelor apartment. Cat and bubbling guppies . . . why scare her?

--Folks. Everyone. Arlo yelled.

--Listen-up. Listen up for a moment. Find a seat. We're safe for now. Wait it out.

People spooled but remained standing. Ghostlike figures coated with ash ran past The Grill's front window, a window in, a window out, a porthole to this new world. Fingers jabbed at 'stupid cell phones.' Parked cars slowly submerged under paper Mache.

Buck pulled a small television down from above the serving window. He turned it toward the awe struck room. All together but each alone, watching now without comprehension. All waiting. For what, no one was sure. Then, as if they heard the sound of a distant starter's gun, each ran head down out into the street stirring the fire ash into a grey paste.

Buck, Jean and Arlo stared at each other then across the empty tables out the window. Each lost in the meaning of it.

--Sorry for butting in, Arlo said, numb. Powerless in the moment.

--You're Jean and Buck. Right?

'White Buck' . . . Buck said, absentmindedly.

--What's happening?

--Don't know.

--Where you living, Arlo? It seemed an odd question.

--East end.

Jean leaned on the exit door.

--I guess we're closed huh?

--Yah. We're closed.

--You heading home Jean?

--Where you living Buck? Arlo asked.

--Upstairs, Buck answered, mesmerized by the television.

--You want to stay here? Now. I mean…instead of going.

--Thanks, but I got my bicycle.

Jean stood bouncing off the back door, the tension in her body building. She needed to go. Her urge to run barely contained.

--How you getin' home Jean? I mean… you live close by? Arlo asked.

--Walkin. We're closed right?

--Yah, yah, we're closed. Go Jean go.

--So I'm the only one staying? *Buck's* voice pulled at Arlo's conscience.

--Jean. Arlo yelled. Wait up. I'll ride you double.

Jean and Arlo pushed into the alley, stopped and stood in the foreign landscape. A new world. The familiar buried. They looked at one another, found strength in each other and walked back into The Grill. Buck stood, transfixed in front of the window. Jean grabbed the telephone, called her apartment, got her grandmother's care worker. Eleanor was alright, she slept, lost to all, but safe. The three of them sat. Ragdolls. Drawn like moths to the flicker of the Television. Images never forgotten. Friendships forged. Something warm between Jean and Arlo.

The Wedding Dress

Vincent eyed the silk wedding dress drifting in the dark waters of the Don Valley River, its river-logged crinoline dragging the depths, netting unsuspecting minnows. He limped over and speared the dress with a sharpened willow stick then dragged it into the mucky shallows. A mass of jellied frog's eggs clung to the virgin dress cocooning a large diamond set in a gold brooch. The brooch was discreetly pinned inside the dress' petite cleavage. He ripped it off, washed it in the flowing water, than held it high to the Toronto sun.

--Ooh-Rah.

He thumb-flipped it into the air, grabbed it down, kissed the diamond then fastened it inside the lapel of his army surplus fatigues.

Vincent whispered.

--My ticket home boys.

His words lost in the din of the old iron bridge's whistling tire grids high above him.

Self-appointed camp boss; Al Crowley, age 52, AKA, Crow—hollered.

--What you got boy?

--Nothing Crow—an old dress is all.

Vince tossed the soggy dress on a thicket of river willows. An image of his younger sister, Jean tugged at him. She stood ankle deep in the Mississippi flood waters wearing a tattered princess dress, clutching her magical fly swatter. Her last words, "take me with you."

--Get rid of it boy.

--It's drying is all, Vince said, we'll use it to start a fire.

--We don't need no girl's dress to start a fire, gimp.

Vince shouldered back and spilled with anger. He tapped the hilt of his waistband knife.

--Careful who you callin' out, Crow. You gonna' take a

dirt nap while you sleepin'.

Crowley scoffed.

--You don't get that leg fixed Vince, you the one taken' the dirt nap, boy. Grab that shipping crate and drag it on up here.

Vince was lean muscle, a twenty one year old US Army reservist, now deserter, from the Treme neighbourhood of New Orleans. He tore a strip of crinoline off the dress then climbed up to their ramshackle encampment under Jimmy Weasell's watchful eye. Weasell lay in his hammock slung between two bridge beams above and off to the side of the camp. Vince sat in one of the lawn chairs corralling the fire pit amid a cobble of shopping carts and cardboard refrigerator boxes strung together to form what the boys called, "The Alamo." He pulled his torn pant leg up and doused his oozing knee with a bottle of alcohol from his gunnysack. Most of the boys were out panhandling and the two found themselves alone.

--How much you owe me, Weasell?

--You know man.

--How much, Jimmy? I want to hear you say it.

--I'm good for it, Vince.

--People are like pigeons, Jimmy—you feed 'em and they shit on you. That what you gonna' do Jimmy?

--I never would, Vince.

--Then forget what you just saw, Jimmy.

The morning sighed on 'till noon. Vince made his decision to leave. His injured leg would be his excuse. Crowley roused from an afternoon slumber down by the river and joined the boys coming back for a meal. He circled Vince looking down on him before sitting across from him.

--Vince. Man that leg stinks. Get it out of here and take that dress with ya.

Vince reached up and grabbed the I-beam and kicked out at Crow. Crow fell backwards and Vince dropped into the soggy fire pit. Crow grabbed a slab of charred firewood. The two locked eyes and Vince's hand touched his knife for all to see.

Someone yelled.

--Hey, hey, Vince—Crow. You don't want to start nothing like that man.

Their loins stilled.

--Crow.

A flurry of hands pointed to the swaying bulrushes across the river. The five men crouched reaching for an assortment of weapons. A valley gang had trashed their camp in the past and "The Alamo Boys" were ready for their return.

Two red-winged blackbirds tumbled midair thrashing their wings over swaying bulrushes on the far side of the river.

Vince laughed.

--You boys are a bit nervous.

Vince lit a cigarette and flipped Crow the finger. He grabbed his gear and hobbled down to the river where he stuffed the dry wedding dress into his rubberized gunnysack and waded out into the shallows. The boys dropped their weapons. Crow waited until Vince was midstream before placing his index finger to his temple. He twisted it back and forth and the boys roared with laughter.

The noonday sun sweated the wind into stillness and Vince stood at the edge of the bulrush maze on the far side of the river listening, scouting a path. The sound of rapid breathing froze him. He inched into the maze, floated his gunnysack beside him then lunged at the noise. A petite shape was plunged into the churning water.

He dragged it up by the hair.

--A girl.

--Let me go. She sputtered.

Vince held her with one hand and swept streaks of dirty hair from her face.

--Let me go.

--Who are you? Vince demanded

--You're hurting me. Let me go.

--What are you doing down here?

--Get off me or I'll scream.

Vince laughed

--For who?

After a paralyzing long moment, she said.

--Toby, my name is Toby. Now let me go.

--You're lying. Vince said. Toby is a boy's name.

--Well I'm not a boy—perv.

--Who are you callin' perv?

--I'm not a boy—now let me go.

--Give me one good reason.

--I don't have to.

--I'm not lettin' go 'till you do.

She cranked her head to one side denying him eye contact and stared a *Grand Canyon* stare at her mother's wedding dress protruding from his gunnysack now set on top of the dense bulrushes. The struggle drained out of her and Vince released her.

--You found my mother's wedding dress.

Vince heard it first—his name, crisp above the sound of a near dozen plunging knees crossing the river.

--Vince. Where you at boy? Jimmy says you got somethin' belongs to us. That right Vince? You got somethin belongs to us? Somethin' off that dress? A diamond brooch maybe?

Vince clasped his hand over Toby's gapping mouth—her eyes bulging.

--Shush. They hear you and we're both done. Promise me you don't yell?

She bobbed her head in wide-eyed agreement. He released her and raised a hush finger to her lips.

--My mother's brooch. You got my mother's brooch?

--Shush. I said.

--I need it. She said.

--Quiet. You'll get us both killed.

--You can't give it to them.

--Hush. Vince flipped open his lapel, showing her the diamond brooch.

--You stole my mother's brooch.

--She, the one threw it away Vince shot back.

--No she didn't.

--How'd it get here then?

--I did. I threw her dress in the river, but I didn't know the brooch was on it.

--Doesn't matter now. Stay down. When I say go, keep your head down and crawl up to that opening in the fence and run as fast as you can.

--I'm not leaving without my mother's brooch.

--You don't get it. You don't get the brooch. You don't get nothin'. You get to go is all.

Toby stood her ground.

--I'm not leaving.

--Don't argue.

--I can't go home without my mother's brooch.

Vince stared at her.

--I can't go home without it, she repeated.

--You stole your mother's wedding dress, now you want it back.

--With the diamond brooch, Toby added

--Now you expect I'll hand it over, just like that, just like I owe you. Damm seagull. You think I'm a free meal?

--No I think you're a stingy bum. You don't care about

anyone, that's why you're a homeless.

--That's right seagull, now get out of here while you still can.

A rustle of dry bulrushes marked The Alamo Boys' location in the marsh.

--Where you at gimp?

Unlike many soldiers, combat stress focused Vince's mind. He reached past Toby trying to grab his gunnysack.

--Toss it to me. Your mother's dress. Toss it.

--No.

--It's wrecked anyway, toss it to me. They getting it and we're gettin' out of here.

He tugged the sack from her grip.

--Run when I toss it. You hear me?

Toby just stared at him.

Vince waited until the boys were within striking distance. He doused the dress and the rubberised gunnysack with a bottle of alcohol from his sack, then lit it.

--No. Toby yelled.

Vince yelled.

--This what you want Crow?

The dress and sack roared into a man-eating fireball igniting the surrounding dry bulrushes and Vince's jacket. He catapulted the burning bag high into the air. The roaring inferno sucked the breath from his mouth and engulfed every living thing. Blinded by the heat and suffocated by the dense smoke, he tore off his jacket and plunged under water taking Toby with him. He grabbed her up and yelled "run *Jean* run" but Toby was past running. Vince lunged back under the spreading flames and dragged her to shore.

--My mother's brooch, Toby retched.

Each stared at the inferno engulfing the marsh, listening to the cries of The Alamo Boys as they dragged each other back across the river.

Vince and Toby lay sprawled on their side of the riverbank.

Vince asked Toby why.

--Why did you steal it?

Toby stared at the sky.

--It didn't matter what I did, she cared more about her wedding than me.

Fire Engines could be heard in the distance as the black smoke engulfed the old steel bridge.

--Why you?

--What? Vince asked.

--Why did you come back for me?

--You, you remind me of someone I should have never left behind—someone special.

Then Vince added.
--Like you.

Waltz Me to the Edge of Love

Anna collapsed. Her swollen ankles rested hard against the Montreal dockside. There she gave birth. This one weighed little more than his placenta but this one would live. His cries echoed across the icy harbour, his fingers coiled like fiddleheads against the cold. Anna believed he snatched his breath from his stillborn sister, but life is for the living and this one, thief or not, screamed for life. She swaddled him in her heavy woollen skirt and held him tight to her aching breast, silencing his cries. This one she would name Mikhail.

His drunken father, Boris, deafened to all but the inner sound of the Gypsy drum, danced around the nativity scene like a performing Russian street bear, clapping his hands. His promises of sobriety forgotten.

High above the joy and sadness, the ship's captain clapped in time with Boris' drunken step—stopping momentarily to allow Boris to kick off his heavy work boots and pinch on a pair of new Italian shoes. A bargain made, the shoes would be payment for the captain's silence but Boris would wear them first—to celebrate the birth of his son.

Amid the throttle and the stench of the merchant fleet, their ship sailed back up the St. Lawrence River lunging against the tidal current. Anna and Boris, illegal immigrants, were left to huddle in the open throat of a shipping container with little more than vodka and hard bread. Anna's prayers were answered when Boris leaned into a trough of heavy sleep, his snoring paused by thunderous passages of foul gas.

She would normally revel in these times of drunkenness—marching around his sleeping body, softy berating him, hiding in the shadows and striking out at him with her broom or ladle, but this time she quieted like dust on cobwebs. Boris must not know of the twin's death. The sound from her bereft heart must not break her lips, and so she set about her child's burial—cleaning and wrapping her tiny body in her babushka, closing her still eyes and parting her lips. There she placed a tiny gold earring, payment for her transport to heaven. She kissed her forehead, covered her face and promised to never forget her. Then she laid her in Boris' empty shoebox.

Boris roused, "What? Anna. What are you doing? What

are you doing with my shoes?"

Anna could not contain herself. "Your shoes. Your shoes you gave to that thieving ship's captain. The box, the box is what we are left . . . to fill . . . with sadness."

"Anna, we had only money for two."

"Yes Boris, only money for two and now we are three Boris? He sleeps now Boris—so must you. You must be strong now Boris, to protect us."

"Finally you gave me a son, Anna."

"Yes Boris, finally I gave you a son."

Boris fell back into the abyss. Anna purposefully tied the box with mischief. His belt—the loss of which she would blame on his drunkenness. She tucked the shoebox in the corner of the garbage dumpster. She would speak of it no more. She returned to the shipping container, pulled the heavy doors closed and cradled her living child. Each spooning back to back to back—there she prayed for a new life in this new country.

As water finds its own level, Anna, Mikhail and Boris found their way into the tiny Russian community in Montreal, where they hid in plain sight. Boris found work in a scrapyard. Anna cooked and cleaned their second-story one-room apartment. Mikhail followed the seasons, first sitting, then to a naked crawl, then to a toddling walk.

It was a Monday evening—the end of a washday. Anna stood before her open alley window—fingerlings of fresh borscht caressed the bib of her apron. Her body wedged onto the corner of the pulsating washing machine while her hands clutched a cloths peg. Her wash line sagged in over her tomato boxes. A sigh of relief parted her lips and she waltzed away from her thoughts of love

Boris ambled up the back alley, his arm around a lean teenage boy with a cast eye. As a young army nurse, she had witnessed these scenes in Afghanistan—a country where men had no access to the willingness of woman. She had no proof, but everyone joked of how a hungry young man could earn extra rations.

She pinned her hair and braced herself—for what, she was not sure. Soon Boris filled the sagging doorframe, his oxbow arm on the pencil-neck youth.

"Anna. One more for soup."

Anna's stomach tightened. She flashed the intruder a furtive glance then turned back to her window box and drove the cloths peg into the moist soil. She raised her fingers to her nostrils and closed her eyes, desperately trying to hold onto her memories of the Russian peat bogs and the arms of her lover.

"Anna. You hear me? One more for soup. This is Tranny. He will be staying with us."

Anna could not believe her ears.

"He will be staying with us," She repeated. "What do you mean?"

"He will be sleeping here, when I am working. We will sleep, when he is working. It is all worked out"

"It is all worked out?" she repeated. "No, it is not all worked out. Where will he sleep? We have no room, no couch."

Boris hesitated. He looked at the floor. "In the bed, when we are awake."

"Are you crazy? In my bed?"

"Anna. The bed will be empty and we need the money."

Anna turned her back to him.

"Anna, he works nights. He will sleep in the day. Nothing to worry about."

Anna tore off her apron and turned to him

"What am I to do while he is sleeping?"

"You can take Mikhail for a walk, a couple of hours. He is a young man, not yet twenty. He needs little sleep.

The image of this youth in her bed awakened every emotion—drunken nights and soldiers pressing down on her—but this was no time to challenge Boris.

Anna marched over to her hot plate and put the kettle on as she did when she needed time to think.

"Did you bring home bread or are we to eat this boy with our borscht?"

"Always with the jokes, Anna. So it is settled then?"

Anna did not speak. She had a long history of holding her tongue—a history of searching soldiers' pockets, taking back some of what they took from her. She did what she had to, convinced herself that the soldiers' pennies would not be missed and they would serve a greater good.

Now, less than two years after their landing in Montreal, she faced the prospects of a stranger sleeping in her bed and learning their secret.

"Anna, watch." Boris caught Tranny's attention.

"Tranny." Boris yelled. He flipped a coin toward Tranny. "Down the street. Get some bread."

The tossed coin dropped through Tranny's closed hands and rolled to the apartment doorway.

Boris laughed.

Anna stood stone-faced.

"What is funny about that?"

"I am showing you he is harmless, Anna. You are harmless, right Tranny?"

Tranny's cast eye left his response in doubt. He turned and slipped out the open door.

Anna turned to Boris, "Are you a fool, Boris?"

Boris stood mute.

"Boris, answer me. You want me to share my bed? This is what you want? Another man in our bed? You turn me into Prostitutki?"

"Anna, he is Muslim. A Muslim Anna. He will not touch you."

Anna set an array of bowls on the table.

"The young men in Afghanistan Boris—weren't they also Muslim?"

Boris turned away. "Anna that was another time. I promise you, he will not touch you. Look at him. A soup bone has more meat."

Anna pulled Mikhail up into her arms.

"Now it is you who jokes Boris."

Anna retreated to her bed behind the alcove curtain and folded laundry.

Boris sat at the kitchen table with a bottle of vodka. The tiny apartment fell silent.

At first sun-up Boris' footsteps echoed down the stairwell. He unchained his bicycle to the sound of a barking dog and rode up the laneway. Tranny lay on the floor. Anna listened for movement, Mikhail beside her.

"Tranny, are you going with him?"

"No, not 'til tonight."

Dead silence.

"Then, cover yourself, I am coming out."

Tranny lay on the floor, wrapped in a torn mover's blanket. Mikhail toddled over to him and offered him a bite of hard bread. Anna caught a glimpse of the welts on Tranny's back. She pulled Mikhail up into her arms, held him tightly. She stepped back from Tranny and unleashed a barrage of prepared questions

"How old are you? Where are you from? How do you know my husband?"

Tranny was quick to respond. "I am nineteen, from Afghanistan."

Anna cut him off. She crouched and looked him in the eye.

"We have no room for you here. You must tell Boris you found another place. "

With that she stood and turned to put the kettle on.

"What are those marks on your back? No, stop.

She stepped toward him, "Why do they call you Tranny?"

Tranny pulled the blanket up to his chin.

"It's just a name. It means nothing."

Anna said, "Everything means something."

Tranny paused.

"Gear box, it means, gear box. . . I like cars."

He dropped the moving blanket to his waist, to distract her. Anna moved to the door. Mikhail stood between her knees, his arms reaching.

"My husband . . . he had his arm around you. That means nothing as well?" Anna ignored Mikhail's cries for attention. "You've told me nothing but lies."

Tranny stood facing the window. "It was because the Russian soldiers offered me money—at night, when I was not translator for them."

Anna walked over to him, whispering. "What do you mean? You mean they used you? She grabbed his shoulder and turned him to face her. "Boris used you?"

"No. No. In Afghanistan . . . during the war. I was translator but I needed money to come to America. They paid me and I ate extra."

"But, you are Muslim."

Tranny stared down at the wooden floor. "I needed to survive—to come, to get here."

Anna asked. "What are those marks on you back?"

"They are nothing--my reminder."

"For what?"

"To treat you with respect."

"Boris did that to you?"

"He is a good man. I will not touch you."

"And still you come to live with us?"

"We do what we have to do."

Anna starred out her window thumbing one gold earring nestled in her apron pocket.

"Yes, we do what we have to do."

JOAN DAULBY

JOAN moved from Vancouver to Whitby, Ontario where she met her husband, Frank. Joan and Frank presently live on their country property north of Barrie.

Joan has been a member of the Mariposa Writers' Group since November, 2006 as well as the founding member of the Writer's Cauldron since March, 2008.

In August, 2007, Joan entered the *Lake Country Literary Lapses* writing contest and placed third in both the prose and poetry categories. Both entries were printed in *Our Literary Lapses*, An Anthology by The Mariposa Writers' Group.

On December 23, 2009, The Packet & Times, Orillia printed Joan's story *Walter Wind Rescues Santa* during their week-long celebration of the Christmas season. Joan has also had an article printed in Woman's Press magazine.

In the past year, Joan has had two books published. Browse through Joan's website at joandaulby.com. and meet Walter, *Walter Wind*, the best wind in the neighbourhood. Walter blows into the lives of children, parents and educators learning about energy conservation, recycling, bullying and Santa Claus.

You'll also meet the *Cool Blues Guy* from the story *Cool Blues* which is dedicated to Joan's grandson, Hunter. Cool Blues tells the story of a seven-year boy who discovers he needs to wear glasses, his concerns and experiences.

These books were released in May, 2011 by Pine Lake Books, West Guilford, Ontario. Pine Lake Books also has four more of Joan's stories bumping shoulders with each other, eager to join *Walter Wind* and *Cool Blues* in the book stores.

Joan has read several of her short stories and chapters from her book at events in the area and has also read her children's books at schools, conferences and writing events.

Although Joan continues to expand her short story library, she is presently working on a book for young adults.

§

Days of Yesterday, Today and Tomorrow

As he left the bedroom, Harry McGarity turned and looked towards his dresser at the brush and comb lined up next to one another. He waited to hear Netti call out, "Harry, don't forget, comb your wavy black locks before you come sit beside me at the window. I want to be able to see those sparkling blue eyes, and I know you'll want the children to see what a handsome man you are as they pass by on their way to school."

However, today the sound of Netti's voice would not be heard. He continued down the hall, leaving the brush and comb untouched. Today when he sat at the window, the rays from the sun would shine between the strands of his now snow-white hair high-lighting the disarray of his mad scientist style. He seldom combed it anymore, didn't see the point of it really.

Sitting mornings at their bay window had been a ritual of theirs ever since the first Saturday in their new home fifty years ago. Every Saturday, they'd begin their weekend with the aroma of breakfast and would load two trays; each filled with a cup of coffee, one egg and two slices of whole wheat toast. They'd rush with trays in hand to their rockers at the bay window where they'd sit and bask in the sun, drink coffee and soak up egg with their toast.

Harry felt so proud sitting beside Netti, her long blonde curls positioned strategically atop her breasts at the perfect angle to the sun, golden shades shimmering with every twist. They reminded him of the long tendrils children drew surrounding the sun—tendrils reaching out to anyone who took the time to marvel at their glory.

But this week Netti would not call out. Harry would sit on his own with his coffee and face the sun of a new day. Today was Monday.

Harry sat slumped at his bay window thinking of all the yesterdays. Never having had children of their own, once they'd retired he and Netti would sit side-by-side at the window every morning, not just on Saturdays. A ritual, yes.

He watched trancelike as the children passed, but never actually seeing them. However, there was Estelle. She was small for her age and like Netti had long blonde curls. In the winter, her curls danced in freedom as they fell from under her hat. On this spring day, Estelle's curls danced as she jumped up and down on the walk in front of him. She was waving her arms, smiling and calling out, "Mr. McGarity! Mr. McGarity! Good Morning!"

At first, Harry didn't see Estelle. He wasn't sure how long she'd been waving at him. He couldn't help but smile and wave back. And so, as one day lead to another, Estelle and Harry McGarity began a ritual of their own.

Then one morning just after Estelle passed by, Harry noticed a green two-door Honda Civic pull up and stop beside her. Estelle leaned over the open window to talk to the driver. He saw her laugh, then get in. He assumed it was one of her friend's parents, but as a "Block Parent," habit made him take note. He tried to read the license plate but could only make out the last four letters "TBYP." He was unable to read the first two—must have been the angle.

"Maybe one's a five or a six. Not sure," he mumbled as he headed to the kitchen to jot down the letters on the grocery pad—all the time thinking he was becoming a paranoid old man.

That evening, there was a knock at the door. Two detectives introduced themselves and handed him a bulletin of a missing child. As he turned the page around to look at the photo, there was Estelle smiling up at him. He was lost for words. He just stood there.

"Sir, do you recognize this child? Have you seen her recently? Sir?"

Harry summoned his voice from the base of his throat. "Yes, that's Estelle. She waved to me this morning as she passed on her way to school. She waves at me every morning."

"Every morning, sir?"

"Why yes. It's our ritual. I sit in my rocker at the window and she waves, jumps up and down and hollers 'Good Morning, Mr. McGarity!' In a sense, we start the day together."

"Estelle never showed up at school today. Did you notice anything unusual, different?"

Harry's eyes widened. He left the detectives standing in the doorway as he rushed down the hall towards the kitchen. "I did! I did! I saw a green car. Now where did I put that grocery list? Here it is! Yes, a green two-door Honda Civic." He shook the note at them as he approached.

"Here, at the top, I jotted down the license plate—well, not all of it. The last four letters. One of the numbers could have been a five or a six. Couldn't quite make it out. I should have known, I should have known. I thought it was a parent. I thought . . ."

The detectives were recording the information Mr. McGarity was giving them.

"Mr. McGarity, thank you. This is the first and only lead we've received. Is there anything else?"

"No, the car drove off down the hill and was gone. I went about my day. I never thought. I really thought . . ." They left Harry standing in his doorway and hurried off.

Harry stepped out onto his front porch and looked down the street to where he last saw Estelle bent over talking through a car window and then laughing as she opened the door and got in. If only he could erase time and start the day again, do something to protect Estelle, do something to change the course of events. Even so, if it wasn't Estelle who disappeared, it may have been some other child. How could he fix that?

Harry watched the Detectives get into their car and then slowly closed his door, blocking out the night. He returned to the couch and picked up his book but just sat and held it. He thought of Estelle and her "good mornings" and couldn't stop the old cliché "if only, if only" from running banners through his mind.

Harry didn't sleep much that night and found himself going to the door and looking out down the street, thinking if he called out her name, she would come running. But no, in dreams only.

As the sun crested the horizon lighting a new day, Harry was already sitting in his chair at the bay window. It seemed like only minutes when he found himself sitting in shadow, the sun now high above his home. A tiredness shrouded him and he left his vigil to nap on the couch.

Hours later, Harry was awakened by a knock at the door. It was the Detectives from last evening. Harry's heart sank.

"Mr. McGarity, we have news. May we come in?" Harry stepped aside and gestured with his arm, inviting them to enter.

"We found Estelle early this morning, unharmed."

"Yes, in dreams." Harry mumbled to himself, his eyes suddenly wet with happiness.

"Thanks to your quick thinking, we worked all night on the

plate numbers you gave us and found the location of the owner not far from here. Apparently, Estelle shoveled his walk this past winter. When he pulled up and offered her a ride, he said he was looking for someone to cut his lawn. She got in because she knew him.

"Estelle, how is Estelle?" Harry spoke unable to keep quiet another minute. "Oh yes, yes. You said she was unharmed, but how is she?"

"She's fine, a little scared but o.k. and is resting at home."

Harry slept well that night. The next morning, as Harry sat in his chair at the window, he saw Estelle and her mother walking towards his home. When he opened the door, Estelle rushed into his arms. Estelle's mother stood wiping her eyes with one hand and balancing a plate of cookies with the other.

"Mr. McGarity, Estelle insisted we bring you some baking. She helped make her favourite cookies to share with you."

"Oh, Mr. McGarity, thank you for finding me."

"Actually, the police did all the work. I just . . . where are my manners? Please, come in."

They all sat at the kitchen table eating cookies and drinking milk. Harry was thankful for the opportunity to spend many more days waving good morning to Estelle.

When Estelle and her mother left, Harry McGarity went to the bedroom, brushed and combed his hair, made a fresh cup of coffee and headed to the bay window. He fixed Netti's shawl just right on the back of her chair and sat down in the sun.

"Netti, my dear, if you were here, you would be proud of me. I have a story to tell. Remember little Estelle? Well . . ."

Miss Dench

A Character Study

When I met Miss Dench, she was already ancient! She had blue-grey hair covered with ocean waves, the popular "do" of the day. Mom said she came with the house. She had been living on the top floor for over thirty years.

The previous owner had built her a cozy one room attic apartment. There was a cot off to one side, a couch on the opposite wall and a huge table and chairs in the centre between them. In the front corner, a small wash basin sat perched on top of curtained cupboards that butted the wall of a three-piece bathroom. The only window was centered above the couch and faced southeast to brighten the room on sunny days.

Mom told me when they bought the house, Miss Dench refused to leave. She was very adamant about staying, and throwing an old lady out into the street just didn't seem proper. So, what else could we do but adopt our attic dweller and accept her as part of our family.

We never heard a peep from her. However as soon as my older brother was off to school, I'd listen for the squeak of the floors as she prepared to leave. I'd scurry to our foyer closet, hide behind the coats and wait for her appearance on the landing.

Miss Dench would come down the stairs clutching a small suitcase in one hand and the railing in the other. Her topcoat was consistently adorned with a colourful scarf and matching gloves. Her shoes weren't fancy, but they looked comfortable and were always properly shined. She swayed a little when she walked and because of her big tummy, she had to sit on the steps to put on her boots.

Initially, I thought Miss Dench left every morning because she lived somewhere else during the day and had to bring a change of clothes. Each day, I watched from my hiding closet as she descended the stairs. Each day, I became more and more curious about her suitcase and what she put in it. As soon as she closed the front door, I'd spring from my closet to soak up the fresh scent that had filled our hallway. She certainly left behind a wonderful smell!

Miss Dench returned home every afternoon around three and once again, I'd squeeze behind the coats to watch her climb the stairs. One day, Miss Dench was halfway up when she turned and spoke in a very soft voice.

"Sarah, I know you're watching from your closet. Would you like to come and have tea and cookies with me? I checked with your mother and she said it would be fine."

This time, I didn't burst into the hallway but slowly slid passed the door nodding my head in confirmation. She smiled the most wonderful smile! It made soft wrinkles at the corners of her eyes and pushed her cheeks out so she looked like my Apple Annie Doll. I hesitated, but the twinkle in her eyes gave me confidence and I scampered up behind her.

Miss Dench placed her small suitcase on the table in the centre of the room and put the kettle on her hot plate. While we waited for the water to boil, she slowly unzipped the top of her case. I kneeled on my chair so I could see inside. I was amazed! My eyes must have been as big as saucers. Miss Dench smiled and softly giggled at my excitement while she carefully began to lift out bottles and jars. Each time she reached for an item, I admired her beautiful long red fingernails.

Once all the jars were sitting before us, Miss Dench informed me they were samples of the fragrances, creams, and nail polish she sold, and that she went door-to-door delivering her orders and demonstrating some of her wares to the "homemakers." If the lady of the house wasn't at home, she didn't mind, she would sell something to the man of the house as a gift for his sweetie. I can still hear her telling me this as she smiled and laughed in delight. She did love her job! She was quite the resourceful woman.

Now I understand why she always smelled so good—from

the glorious creams she put on her face and hands. To this day, when I walk through the cosmetic section of a store, I sniff a scent—a Miss Dench scent. I will never forget our adopted attic dweller and her wonderful smell.

Miss Dench in the centre surrounded by her adoptive family.

Vienna Vanilla

It felt strange driving to our new office on the edge of town. When I learned management was going to renovate the old McDougall residence at the base of Mount Isabella, I was thrilled. Now that we've moved in, I'm not so sure. It's nice, lots of space but isolated, lonely. Although our downtown office was only ten feet wide and was squeezed between the drug store and the corner variety, our large front window gave us opportunity to watch the daily street scenes unfold. I'm certainly going to miss being audience to these little vignettes and the scurry of shoppers hustling from store to store.

Early this morning on my way to work, I stopped at "Where Friends Meet" to pick up our usual Tuesday coffees. When I looked up the street, I saw our old shingle with a peel and stick "FOR RENT" notice pasted diagonally across our lettering. Memories fluttered through my mind and a yearning for what used to be, surfaced and then subsided. This Tuesday was our first coffee meeting at the McDougall home and it would be a celebration.

I pushed open the front door with my foot, my hands full of goodies. I set the box of coffees off to the side of my desk and bestowed the centre location for our special treat of the day, hidden in a paper bag waiting to be crinkled open. The sun shining through the entrance this crisp January morning was invitation enough for me to venture out to the steps of the old Victorian porch to await the arrival of my coffee buddies. The new Homeland Insurance sign stood proudly at the base of the stairs announcing our new location.

In the distance, the town of Emerald Green stretched before me--storefronts and offices lined up on either side. The main street wide and bustling, cars angle-parked; reminiscent of western towns of long ago, horses tethered to their hitching posts.

Tuesday was Joe's day off--the day he drove Jackie to work, the morning Jackie and I sat and shared a brief visit with her hubby before he headed to ski the slopes of Mount Isabella--the gentle mountain that watched over the town of Emerald Green, keeping everyone safe. At least, that was how the story went.

I looked up at the blue sky spotted with floating white clouds, a strong contrast to the weather report this morning, and wondered how they could go from white to heavy gray within the next few hours. It must be a mistake. I knew Mount Isabella would hold the clouds back as long as she could, but once they pushed around her peak, they would drop and release their snowy bundle.

I shivered and got up to head inside. As I turned, the Stills' green SUV with skis strapped to the roof emerged from between the trees at the base of the hill. I waved, and waited for them to pull into our lot.

"Hi, you two! I was about to check our brews. They may need to be nuked."

"Mornin' Trish!"

If I didn't know better, I would have expected to see two westerners with ten gallon hats standing in front of me. Instead, I saw a vertically challenged lady dressed to the hilt with a red hat plunked atop her head and a tall skinny fellow dressed in skiing gear with goggles perched atop his head.

"Aren't you two a sight to behold," I laughed. "Now, let me guess. Jackie, you're going skiing and Joe, you're off to the office. Doing things together, separately. Right?" Their blank stare told me it was taking a minute for them to catch up. They surveyed each other and shrugged their shoulders.

"I need my coffee!" Jackie said as they climbed the steps. She had the annoying habit of ignoring my wit.

We entered the office to the welcoming aroma of coffee from our take-outs, and Jackie crinkled open our treat. We devoured the fresh strawberry muffins, drank our java and bid farewell to Joe.

"Joe, don't forget to be home by two for the washer repair guy," Jackie hollered after him.

"I'll be there. I only want a few hours skiing before the storm arrives."

Sure enough by noon, the white clouds and sun were rapidly disappearing. "Trish, do you suppose the weatherman was right? Look at those clouds coming over the top of Isabella."

"Well, they have to be right some of the time." I joined Jackie at the window and we watched as dark gray shadows appeared, the clouds bumping and breaking through Isabella's peak.

Time passed quickly. The storm took shape around us and by mid-afternoon, the wind was beating large gusts of snow against the windows. The day had taken on an early evening grayness, cold and foreboding. Jackie's anxiety was rising. She tried reaching Joe at home, but there was no answer.

I watched as she paced back and forth to the bay window. Each time she pressed her nose against the cold glass and squinted— as if squinting would make a better sight line between the snowflakes. Then she'd turn away, leaving two nose-breath circles on the glass and march back to her desk, stiletto heels clacking on the hardwood. If it weren't for her four inch spikes, she'd barely reach five feet. After listening to the rhythm of her pacing for the past couple of hours, I could have picked her out anywhere--clack, clack, clickety-clack, clack. Many times I've tried to imitate her stride, but have always failed.

"Jackie, Jackie Stills," I said as she sat at our abutting desks. "You are quite the show. Why don't you relax and wait? Mimic your name would ya . . . be 'STILL.' Joe WILL be here!"

"I admit, he's got me nervous. He should have answered my calls. And, now he's late . . . I don't like it when he's late— especially in bad weather." Jackie fidgeted with the things on her desk then slowly cracked each of her long fingers. Every time she raised her head and looked towards the window she'd fling her long hair back over her shoulder.

"He'll be here!" I reassured her.

"I'm not sure . . . This time, with the storm and all, and not being home when he should be, I'm really worried." Jackie absently took a strand of her dark brown hair and twisted it into a tight spiral. Unable to sit for a moment more, she jerked to her feet, trotted her stilettos back to the window and scrunched her nose against the pane.

"Jackie, please . . . sit! The good news, Joe gets to drive

to the office on all the "down" mountain roads. It's your trip home and getting up all those windy roads, you should be worrying about."

Jackie turned and glared at me. My smile didn't do a thing to ease her anxiety nor to stop the daggers from her piercing dark eyes. Whenever Joe was late, I could definitely expect retaliation from her little gold atomizer. And now, on top of being late, Jackie's calls home were left unanswered.

Jackie stomped back to her desk balancing her full-figure frame atop her "steepled" shoes, grabbed her purse and started pulling out the contents. Finally, out came the familiar gold Vienna Vanilla perfume bottle—her indication of extreme anxiety. Jackie pulled off the lid, placed her middle finger on top of the "squirter" and pushed the nozzle three times as her spangle-laden arm circled her head. The fragrance from the mist immediately filled the entire office with the "Jackie" smell—the smell of a freshly baked angel food cake. The aroma exuded was definitely her calling card and warned strangers of her presence.

"Now you've done it! Not only do we have to sit and wait for Joe to arrive, now we have to sit hungry at the end of a long day and wish we could eat cake! I have to admit though, your Vienna Vanilla does mask the musty smell of this old house. Or should I say, recently renovated NEW office space?"

"Ha! Ha! You're so funny! I think I'll take one more look."

"Of course you will."

"He's here, he's here! I can see headlights coming from the base of the mountain."

"Told yah he'd make it."

Jackie ignored my banter and began putting her purse back together and tidying her desk. She gave one last scrutinizing glance at her work area before heading to retrieve her coat and hat from the hooks at the back door.

It was always a delight to watch Jackie emerge in her laced high heeled snow boots and fancy camel coat topped off with her favourite red hunter's cap that Joe gave her at Christmas. The cap was for their snowshoeing treks through the bush, but she wore it everywhere! Today, instead of having the ear flaps tied neatly on top, I knew she'd have them flapping freely, dangling against her ears or even worse, because of the storm she'd have them tied securely, the laces forming a large bow under her chin.

I already teased her far too much about the image she presented, and today was not a good day to remind her. I kept my thoughts to myself and began straightening up the disarray on my desk.

The double beep from a horn indicated Joe had pulled into the driveway. I could hear him clumping his boots as he crossed the veranda, trying to knock off as much snow as possible before entering. The door burst open and in came Joe and the weather. He grabbed the edge of the door, shouldered it with all his weight and slammed it shut, sealing out the intensity of the storm.

"Hi, Joe! How was the drive? Did the washer get fixed?" I asked, continuing to organize my day's work. When he didn't answer, I looked up and found him inching his way along the hall runner, nose raised towards the ceiling, sniffing.

"Did someone bake a cake?" he asked, winking at me.

Jackie stomped in from the back, bristling and shouting at Joe.

"Why didn't you answer my calls? Why have you let me worry all afternoon? Huh?"

Joe was stunned. His light-hearted demeanour quickly vanished.

"I didn't hear any phone."

"Well, I must have called a dozen times."

"Easily," I confirmed.

"Gee, Jackie, I'm sorry. The repair guy cancelled. He didn't want to travel up the mountain with the storm coming. Look at me Jackie. My face has grease on it because I spent the day in the basement trying to fix the machine myself. As you know, I'm no repair guy. However--and I say this lightly--I do think I got it fixed. We can put a load in as soon as we get home. We'll be in clean clothes tomorrow!"

"Ummm . . . sorry." Jackie reached out and gave Joe a hug. She licked her finger and rubbed a dirty smudge off his cheek. "Let's get on our way. I won't relax until we're home."

"That makes two of us," I said and by the look on their faces, they had totally forgotten all about me. "Not to worry, I'll close up the office. This is one night I'm happy to be living in town. When you get home, call me!"

"I will." Jackie turned to go but before heading out the door, she surprised me and returned to give me a hug.

Realizing how fierce the weather had become, I decided to leave my desk "as is" and get going myself. I grabbed my clothing from the back, turned out the lights and headed to my car--now covered with at least a foot of snow and did the fastest clean-off job I had ever done.

I jumped into my frozen little igloo. I was so eager to get started I revved the engine and backed into the bank on the other side. I was stuck! I revved the engine repeatedly, rocking the car backwards and forwards but to no avail. I remained stuck. "Great!" I yelled pounding the steering wheel.

I dashed back to the warmth of the office. Tonight was going to be a long one. At least the hydro was working and the gas-fired hot water rads would continue to supply good heat. Sleeping was going to be difficult--no comfy chairs or couches had been moved in yet, only our desks and filing cabinets. Living on my own, and with no relatives, I resolved to snuggle in.

I pulled three office chairs together for a bed and laid my coat on top. The warm rads were perfect for drying my hat and gloves and once dried, I'd wrap them in my scarf to use as a pillow. I tried calling Jackie and got a dead line. I made a mental note to try again later. Storms have proved to be the masters over cell phone reception.

No television, no books. I decided to catch up on some work to pass time. Hopefully the snow plough would be here soon and I'd be saved from sleeping on wooden chairs--maybe the floor would be a better choice.

About an hour later, I saw the plough heading full speed towards Mount Isabella. I thought it would probably take at least an hour to do the mountain road--I'd be able to flag him down on his way back. I put on my boots, ready to run outside once I heard the plough scraping along.

Sure enough, on one of my window checks, I saw the plough coming towards the office. The blade was spraying snow far into the ditch. I grabbed my coat and ran out waving and yelling--even though I knew the driver couldn't possibly hear me over the noise of the plough. He flashed his lights in recognition and I waded through the snow to the safety of the porch. It was hard to believe that only this morning I sat on this very porch basking in the sun.

I couldn't tell from where I stood who was driving, Harvey or Liam, but when our lot was cleared, the door opened and a pair of long legs reached out for the ledge to climb down, and I knew it was six-foot Harvey.

"Hey, Trish, is that you?"

"Hey, Harvey! Am I glad you saw me. As you can see, I'm stuck--backed into the snow bank earlier. I was about to try sleeping on chairs."

"Chairs? Wouldn't you rather be home in your own bed? Let's see if I can get you out." Harvey dug out my rear wheels while I brushed off the new snow and cleared my windows.

"O.K., Trish. Give it a try." With Harvey pushing, and me revving forward, I was out.

"Thanks, Harv. You didn't see anyone stuck up there on the mountain road, did you? Joe picked up Jackie around five and I haven't been able to reach them."

"No, no one. They were probably so glad to be home, they never checked their messages."

"Yah, you're probably right. Thanks for the help. I'll turn off the lights and lock up. I should be fine now."

Harvey climbed back into his heated cab and was off. He had the rest of the town to plough out before morning.

Thanks to Harvey, maneuvering the roads was easy--he blazed the trail, I followed and was home in no time. I was so glad to be warm and safe. I jumped into bed and was asleep within minutes, never giving Jackie another thought.

I arrived late at the office the next morning, expecting to see Jackie sitting at her desk, tapping her watch. The lot was deserted--no SUV, no tracks in the fresh snow, nothing. I tried her phones again. Her cell was still dead, so I left another message on her home phone. By noon I was really getting worried. I called Fred at the Police Station and filled him in.

"Trish, why don't I take a drive up to the Stills and see what's going on. Maybe their lines are down up there. More likely, they had a rough night and slept in."

"That'd be great, Fred. Thanks." It wasn't even a half hour later when my phone rang.

"Hi, Trish. The Stills SUV isn't in the driveway and no one answered the door. When I came back down, I checked for any vehicles stuck in the ditches--nothing. It wouldn't hurt to have Eric from our Canine Team, take his dog, Trace, for a wander up Isabella way. With all the snow that was dumped through the night, maybe I missed them."

"Missed them? Do you mean they may have spent the night in their SUV? It's my fault. I should have let you know last night when I couldn't reach them."

"Trish, how could you know? Let me call Eric. He and Trace can meet me at the base of the mountain."

"I have a scarf of Jackie's, Trace can sniff if that'll help."

"No, that's o.k. Trace is trained to follow the last scent. If the Stills are anywhere on or near that road, he'll find them."

I said a silent prayer to Isabella to keep them safe--Jackie often said Isabella watched over them as they slept. Like Jackie, I started pacing from my desk to the window--back and forth, back and forth. Finally, I moved my chair to the window, rested the phone on the sill and waited. Fred went by shortly after my phone call. Ten minutes later, I watched Eric's canine wagon pass and I returned to my desk to wait for news.

I heard the sirens before I saw them. Both rescue units disappeared behind the trees at the base of Mount Isabella. I couldn't wait any longer. I ran out and jumped in my car.

When I arrived at the hill, the only vehicles were Fred's cruiser and Eric's canine wagon. Not close enough. I would have to go further up. I was approaching the switch back when I saw the fire truck and ambulance parked off to the side. Fred saw me coming and came clumping down towards me, waving his arms and motioning for me to stop.

"Fred, Fred!" I hollered out. "What's going on? Is it Jackie and Joe?"

"Stay put, Trish. Yes, it's the Stills. When the plough went by last night, it totally covered their car. That's why I missed them. Trace started to dig frantically at the bank and there it was, their SUV on its side against a big tree. Joe's door's stuck. They're both inside. We're using the Jaws of Life to get them out."

"They've been there all night? They've been there all night? How are they? Are they o.k.? Can they talk to us? Fred, tell me how they are!"

"Take it easy, Trish. There was no way you could have known. Strange though, when they cracked open the door, all we could smell was cake. No wonder Trace found them so quickly. It smelt like a bakery in there."

I couldn't help but smile. "That's Jackie's perfume. She used it . . . often."

"As soon as we get them loaded into the ambulance, you can follow to the hospital. They'll be able to give you a full report from there."

All the way to the hospital, I fretted and talked to myself. I hurried through the doors to the reception area.

"I'm a friend of the Stills, Joe and Jackie Stills. They've just been brought in by ambulance. Could you have someone check on them, see if I can go back?"

"Of course. Wait here." The receptionist went through the doors to the emergency area. After what seemed like forever, the doors swung open and a nurse walked towards me.

"Are you Trish Simmons, Jackie's friend?"

"Yes."

"Come with me, Jackie's asking for you. You should know, Joe didn't make it. He was bleeding internally. There was nothing we could do."

"Nooo, no. Jackie . . . have you told her yet?"

"Not yet. Once we get her warmed up and stable, we'll let her know. She knows she can't talk with Joe right now. She's a strong one. Joe had a sleeping bag over him. No doubt, it was Jackie who covered him. Good thing she had on a warm coat and hat, probably kept her alive."

I approached her bed as quietly as possible, my coat swishing with every step.

"Hi, Jackie, it's me, Trish." I leaned over to caress her forehead and felt the heat from the pre-warmed blankets. "With all these blankets, you'll be warm in no time. How are you doing?"

Jackie's eyes fluttered, opened briefly and closed. I pulled the chair over and reached for her hand. I sensed she knew I was beside her. Someone told me it was comforting to talk to patients even when they're sleeping, so I told her all about being stuck, trying to sleep on my chair bed, and being pushed out by Harvey.

Finally, a couple of nurses came around to get Jackie settled into a room.

"Here, take her boots and follow us. Once we get her settled, you can stay with her as long as you want." I followed them to a room with a large sunny window. Jackie would like this--she'd be able to look outside.

I stayed and watched her sleep--the sleep of the exhausted. The nurses came and went, checking her vitals. Lunch time was long gone and I decided to search out a cup of coffee. The nurses said if

Jackie woke while I was gone, they'd let her know I'd be back.

Upon my return, one of the nurses took me aside.

"The doctor was in to see Jackie while you were away and told her about Joe. She's waiting for you."

I opened the door to Jackie's room--half wishing she was asleep and half wanting to comfort her. When she saw me, she broke down into uncontrollable sobbing.

"Trish, Joe's gone. Joe's gone! What am I going to do? I yelled at him about the washer. I yelled at him to slow down but he was afraid if he did, we'd never make it. We were skidding in circles. I was so scared. We hit the cliff and slid off the road."

I rushed to her side, scooped her into my arms and hugged and shushed her until she finally stopped.

"Trish, I covered him up and everything. I thought he'd be fine. He wasn't dressed very warmly. I covered him with our sleeping bag." Jackie said, her voice desperate.

"Jackie, there was nothing you could do. Joe was injured inside. You did the right thing trying to keep him warm." I reached into my pocket and handed her the Vienna Vanilla bottle. "They found this on the floor."

"I couldn't get Joe to wake up. I kept spraying it so he'd know I was right there with him."

"Well, that's how Trace found you. You know, Trace. Eric's search dog. When Trace smelled your perfume, he went right to you."

Jackie's sobbing had stopped but the tears kept coming. I climbed onto the bed next to her and cradled her until she fell asleep, her little gold bottle clutched securely in her hand.

I left the hospital in a trance. The next few days were going to be tough. When I returned in the evening, Jackie was sitting up staring at a full tray of food.

"I can't eat, Trish. The pastor was in and we were talking about Joe's funeral. It's going to be on Saturday. I know, it's fast but like you, we don't have any family and what family we do have are so far away. Both our parents are gone. You are the closest family I have."

"I know, and you are mine. Jackie, they say you can go home tomorrow. Come stay with me for a while. Would you do that? Stay with me? I'd really like to have you with me."

Jackie nodded. We talked all evening about Joe, his love for skiing, what a good father he would have been, and how he just may have fixed the washer. Whenever we stopped talking, Jackie would drift off. She didn't want me to leave but visiting hours were ending and I edged away the next time she fell asleep.

I helped Jackie through the next few days. The funeral was small but the room was filled with flowers from all those who knew Joe--skiing buddies, town friends and long lost relatives across the country. Jackie didn't know all his buddies but Joe had told them all about his Jackie.

Jackie stood proudly beside Joe's coffin and in the last moments when she said her final goodbye, she reached into her pocket, pulled out her little gold bottle and placed it in Joe's hand.

"Joe, this is for you. Spray my Vienna Vanilla every now and then and remember me. Keep safe 'till I see you again."

DOLL   BEE

ALICE de MUNNIK

ALICE was born in the Netherlands and immigrated to Canada in the early 1950s. She spent her formative years in Orillia. The next phase of her life took her to careers in Toronto and Vancouver, before returning to Orillia in 2004.

Although Alice is now semi-retired, her work career has included being a legal secretary, trainer and supervisor in large law firms in Toronto and Vancouver, a teaching master at Seneca College, a lecturer at Ryerson University and a life issues therapist. She currently does editing work and since 2005 has been the editor of the anthology created each year by participants in the Orillia Library Lifescapes Programme. For the past ten years, Alice has taught classes to people who want to write their family stories and hopes to start a fiction writing class in the near future. Alice has finished her memoir entitled "Assimilating" and is hoping to have it published in the near future. Alice has also completed a novel, which is at the revision stage, and two collections of short stories. As well, she had completed a non-fiction book called "Lessons from the Men I Have Known."

In August of 2005, Alice won the gold prize for short fiction at the Lake Country Literary Lapses Festival for her short story *Dancing at Mel Levine's* and the gold prize for poetry in August 2007 for her poem *A Long Journey Home.*

Buster

"One more time, class!" Sister Verity says. "Let me hear you soft and sweet as if you're pulling butterscotch from your mouth." Sister wants us to recite "Trees" by Alfred Joyce Kilmer. I wonder if Mr. Kilmer is still alive? I think he's probably dead and in heaven so he can be closer to his trees and to God. I wonder whether heaven has one section for adults, one for children, another for animals and trees and a really small one for nuns.

I'm not paying much attention because I'm thinking of Buster. I wonder if I'll see him when I go to heaven and if he'll still know me. He didn't mean to get Mrs. Russell's rabbits all upset. All he was doing was playing with them. They were cooped up in their pen all day with not much to do but eat lettuce and look at places they can't go because they're rabbits and they're in a cage. I'd think they'd want a nice dog like Buster to come along and make something of their day.

"Louder class", Sister says. "All together now."

I think that I shall never see
A poem lovely as a tree
A tree whose hungry mouth is pressed
Against the earth's sweet-flowing breast

Sister beats her pointer on the top of each desk as she walks up and down the rows. She pinches the back of my arm as she walks past my desk. I quickly join in with the other girls and boys in my class.

Trees were Buster's favourite things. He used them to mark his territory. Sometimes he'd rub his back against the trunk to scratch himself. I liked it when he'd jump at the bottom branches and try to bite off the leaves. He'd try and try, but he could never get hold of them. I think if he could have, Buster would have lived in a tree just so he could look down on all the other dogs and do nothing but eat leaves all day.

In the winter, Buster and I would go sleigh riding on the big hill in the Valley. It's really the first bush, but everyone calls it the Valley. I'd get one of the Trent Valley Bakery cardboard boxes that the bread came in every week and use it as my sleigh. My best friend, Susan, and I would hop on the cardboard and slide down into the Valley. Buster would wait until the very last minute and when he saw us coming, he'd jump on the back. Sometimes, he'd jump on Susan and me because we were going so fast and he'd fall right on top of us. When that happened, we'd laugh all the way to the bottom of the hill, trying to hold on, with Buster barking as loud as he could to show everyone how much fun he was having.

Buster loved coming to the second bush with me. The two of us would go off by ourselves, away from the house. He'd fetch sticks and anything I'd throw at him. Sometimes he'd catch them in the air when he was feeling really good. My brother, Billy, said that Buster is good enough to go on the Ed Sullivan Show, but I don't think Buster would want to go all the way to New York City on the bus just to be on Ed Sullivan for a couple of minutes.

To get to the second bush, we first had to go through the Valley behind our house. As we walked, Buster would spot a rabbit or a field mouse. His ears would stand up and he'd be all at attention. He'd growl and tell the animals that this was his Valley and they'd better watch out. All I'd have to say is 'come on Buster, let's go boy' and he'd leave what he was growling at and trot along beside me on the trails that had been carved out of the Valley over the years.

The best time to go to the second bush was in the Fall when I'd go to get leaves for my school projects. Buster would come along and guard me as we left the Valley, crossed the highway and went further and further into the second bush to get the really good leaves: the poplars, the red and silver maples, the basswood with its big round leaves, the sumac trees with their red, pear-shaped velvet flowers and the birch trees that invited me to take a piece of their bark to show Sister Verity. Sister isn't allowed to go into the bush or anywhere else unless another nun goes with her. My brother, Billy, says that nuns are sacred and they have to be careful because some people might hurt them if they go out alone. I don't know about that. What I do know is that Sister Verity would never let anyone do anything to her without giving them a good smack on the head first.

Buster was my advance scout on these leaf-gathering trips. He'd check to see if there were any people or other animals in the second bush that might hurt me. Once I found the trees I was looking for, Buster would take off and come back with empty bottles, crumpled cigarette packages, old bicycle tires, paper bags and anything else he could dig up for me to look at.

Once I'd collected all the leaves I needed, Buster and I would make our way back. We'd take the long way around Victoria

Point, just in case anyone saw me and told Dad about where I'd been. Then we'd walk down Forest Avenue and turn left at Franklin Street for the last block home.

When I got near the house, I'd hide the leaves under my jacket so Dad wouldn't see them. Mom knew where I'd been, but she'd never tell. I'd whisper to her that I needed waxed paper and could I use the iron. She'd whisper back, 'wait until your Father's gone to bed'. That night I'd set up the ironing board quietly so Dad wouldn't hear the squeaking of the rusty hinges as I pulled the legs straight out. I'd lay the sheet of waxed paper on top of each leaf and watch as the heat from the iron transferred the wax. Mom would peek over from time to time and smile at what I was doing as she darned the socks in her basket. I'd hold up the stiff waxed leaves so she could have a look.

Late at night was the only time Mom ever let me sneak Buster into the house and then only for a few seconds because he got so excited and made so much noise slapping his tail against everything. Most times, Buster lived and slept under the porch in a box that I'd put some old blankets in so he wouldn't get cold.

After Dad shot Buster for playing with Mrs. Russell's rabbits, I wanted to wrap him up in the blankets from his box and carry him to the second bush and bury him there. Just him and the trees. He'd have a place where Dad would never kick him or shoot him again. Dad had other ideas. Billy told me later that Dad must have been a little bit sorry for shooting Buster. After he dug the hole in the backyard and threw Buster in, Dad put a couple of flowers from Mom's garden on top.

No one at my house talks about Buster any more. Even Billy doesn't want to hear stuff about Buster. He says it's time to stop all that talking and crying and get a new dog or maybe a cat would be better 'cause they have nine lives.

I had another dream about Buster last night. Buster was sitting in one corner of heaven looking down on me and the other dogs and getting fat on leaves. He was having some really nice dog dreams and listening to a new poem the angels have written for him:

We think that we will never see

A dog as beautiful as Buster is...

Waiting for the Call
(An excerpt from the Memoir, "*Assimilating*")

By the time Easter comes that year, Sister Mary Blanche is close to convincing me that I should become a nun. Taking the veil is the best thing a Catholic girl can do. Mom would like it, too, since one of Dad's sisters, Tante Marie, is a nun in a strict order in Holland. It would be nice if there was a nun in Canada.

Sister says that if God means for me to be a nun, I will get the call. I wait and wait, but nothing happens. Maybe I'm not hearing God or He is speaking too softly.

To be a nun, you have to be humble and accept the vows of chastity, poverty and obedience; otherwise, you will not be worthy. We are poor because Dad only earns 77 cents an hour at The Canada Wood Specialties for himself, Mom and us nine kids, so there's no problem with the vow of poverty. I don't know much about chastity. It's what grown-ups do behind locked doors and there's a lot of heavy breathing. Mom always says that she'll tell me about sex when I'm older. I don't know when I'll be old enough, but I do believe that chastity won't be much of a problem either. Keeping two of three vows is pretty good I think.

It is the vow of obedience that probably made God decide against me. In my heart, I am not an obedient girl. I don't agree with what grown-ups say and do and tell children to do or not do. I also think that Sister Mary Blanche isn't a very good nun. She always says mean things to us and gives us the strap. She blames her pupils for giving her nerves a bad time and causing her back pain. What really is a surprise is when Father Doyle or one of the other priests at Guardian Angels Church comes to visit our class and Sister Mary Blanche's face turns bright red. I thought nuns weren't supposed to blush when a man comes into the room, even if he is a priest. I often wonder if Sister listens to Mother Superior at the Mother House on Penetang Street. Does she ever break her vow of obedience?

Sister also tells us that to be a good nun, you have to give up all vanity. When you are a nun, you will not care one bit about your appearance or whether your hair looks nice because no one will see it. You won't be able to wear lipstick or use nail polish or wear jewellery, other than a wedding ring, which shows that you are married to God. The black and white habit, with the veil, bib and wimple, will be the only clothing you will wear once you take your final vows. Above all else, Sister says that as a nun, you will never be able to look in a mirror again. When I walk to school every day up Mississaga Street, I always look in the showcase windows to make sure my hair looks neat and I don't have a dirty face. Sister doesn't like untidy girls.

Having God as a husband is a problem for me. I don't understand how that will work out with God having so many brides, especially since the Catholic Church only allows one marriage and no divorces. And you will never have children, Sister says. After thinking this through, it makes sense because how would it sound if I had a baby and when she asks who her father is, I'd have to say it was God. Aren't we all God's children? Besides, it would be sacrilegious to say that God is my husband and the father of my children. I'd have to go to confessions and tell Father Doyle I'd committed a mortal sin or two.

After a few more months of thinking hard on the matter, I finally accept that I will never become a nun. I'm not humble enough. It's a good thing that I didn't say anything to Mom and Dad because then I would have to explain why I changed my mind. My Grandmother de Munnik in Holland will be upset that there won't be a Canadian granddaughter turned into a nun. My grandmother believes that Canada is a heathen country filled with people who seldom go to church. It also has red Indians riding the plains and cowboys who do nothing all day but lasso cows, drink whiskey and sing country songs. But, as my oldest brother always says, what they don't know won't hurt them.

It isn't long after I decide that I'm probably not fit to be a nun, that Mom receives a letter from Holland announcing that Tante Marie is no longer a nun. Tante Marie asked the Pope to let her out of the convent. Her Mother Superior in Holland was afraid that Tante Marie's strange behaviour was due to her having a brain tumour. If she stayed in the convent much longer, they felt she would go crazy and die. Mom says that the tumour grew because there were too many rules and all that praying wasn't good for Tante Marie.

Will she still die, I ask Mom, as she reads the letter out to me.

No, I don't think so. They got her out just in time. The Pope gave Tante Marie his special blessings and said she could leave and go back to her family. But there is no one in the family who can take her.

Couldn't she just get married and go live with a husband somewhere in Holland and have her own place?

That remains to be seen, Mom answers. No one knows what Tante Marie suffered in that cloister. No one knows what it will be like living with a nun who is no longer a nun. Maybe she's crazier than we think.

If going into the convent made Tante Marie sick, then maybe it's better not to contemplate religious life. By the end of the school year, I have totally given up on hearing the call and being a nun. It seems better that way.

As for Tante Marie, within two years of getting out of the convent, she met and married the first of two husbands, both named Willem. From the letters Mom receives from Tante Marie, it looks like being a nun didn't ruin her chances of being a wife, although she never had children with either of her two husbands. I wonder what the Catholic Church thinks about that?

The Reluctant Lover

I came to you unknown, as you did to me
I was looking for something to make a difference to my life
Little did I know it would be someone
At first you were distant, aloof and I was a little afraid
You were like an impenetrable fortress
All you were was hidden inside
I don't consciously remember when
For I was not yet aware
But I found myself reaching out to you in unspoken words
Communicating with my senses
I wanted to get past your defences
You were an enigma, a closed book
Yet, I was hopeful. I liked the cover
The fabric, I thought, had worn well
Then, one day, a tiny ray of light broke through
So small, yet, so intense
It pierced the fortified veil of your resistance
Little by little the stones crumbled
Your feelings started to take shape and breathe
They were like the first flowers in Spring
Delicate, shaky and cautious, but there
When they took shape and bloomed, I couldn't say
Was I the first? Or did I just encourage
In you what had lain dormant
Shrinking in on itself with no hope of expression
Those feelings long kept buried
Burst forth, but you kept them to yourself
You didn't want to share them
You said they would come out wrong
That you would appear foolish
That if you used the words
The sounds would not belong
Perhaps you fear that I won't return them
Or, maybe, you fear that I will

That if you let your emotions flow free
They will never be as pure or vibrant as now
As they lie in limbo waiting for immaculate redemption
As you walk away from me
And return to your solitary, safe existence
I know I will not grieve for you
Or try once more to break your self-imposed silence
That cannot bear the heart touches I want to give
For I know there will be another
Who is a stranger as yet, waiting for me
To share what he is, what he was yesterday
And what he will become tomorrow
I just hope he will not keep me waiting too long.

MICHELLE DUFF

MICHELLE was born in 1939 in Toronto, Ontario, Canada. She has lived most of her life in Toronto, although in the 1960s she spent eight years travelling parts of Europe and one year in California, U.S.A. In 2000, she moved from Toronto north to the wilds of Central Ontario and the town of Coldwater. She lives in a small winterized cottage on two acres of rocks, trees, bugs and bears, 100 metres from Lake Otter, where she has a dock and a canoe. She is often seen swimming in the lake or canoeing around the gentle waters in summer checking on the beaver lodges and heron nests or cross-country skiing or skating across the ice in winter. She shares her life with two dogs and three cats and whatever other wild creatures are in need of company.

Since her early teen years, Michelle has had many magazine articles published on a variety of topics, but only recently has she taken the craft more seriously. Michelle now has six books in print and is presently working on her seventh.

Michelle is also a talented wildlife photographer.

All, Save One

The first attack occurred early one morning. I awoke to a racket of cackling and honking like the evening rush hour I thought I'd left behind in downtown Toronto. The noise was deafening. And then the dog started barking in defence of what she now considered her back yard. Out on my lovely lawn were at least twenty Canada geese, both adults and adolescent goslings. They'd taken over the bottom ten metres of my manicured grass and show-quality flower beds.

I had no problem with them eating the grass; it was what they left behind I disliked. What came out of their back ends didn't seem at all proportional to what went in the front. Canada goose exhaust does little to fertilize grass and leaves a brown stain wherever it lands. And the bottom ten metres above the river looked like someone had aerated my beautiful lawn. White and grey curls of goose excrement covered every patch of green.

I grabbed two pots sitting in the drainage tray by the sink and ran down towards the river shouting and banging the pots together. Foolish exercise, during the ensuing exodus it rained goose excrement at an alarming rate. To my distorted eyes, the extra deposit completely covered the bottom ten metres of grass, including two beds of newly bloomed roses. I was not happy.

As the geese had come up from the river I erected a small fence along the river's edge, thinking it would keep them away. For some reason it escaped me that Canada geese can fly.

The next morning, perhaps the same flock of geese or maybe another flock, or maybe two separate flocks, I don't know, but a huge goose population had settled on my bottom ten metres of precious grass. Were geese now drawn to this spot, like a cat who pees on the rug then considers it fair game to continually use this spot as a personal urinal?

"The dog," I whispered to myself. "Hee, hee; sweet revenge." Sara took off down the yard in record time. The flock scattered, leaping into the air faster than a jet fighter plane off the flight-deck of an aircraft carrier.

Having extricated the trespassers from her yard, Sara reared up on her hind legs and gave one last bark as if to say, "And don't come back, or else." All the geese were gone, all save one.

A young gosling, new to the world of fear, or perhaps confused by the rush of air of ascending birds, had run for the security of the river and became entrapped in the wire mesh of the newly erected fence.

Sara turned her attentions toward the young goose struggling to free itself from the wire. Like an athlete savouring her moment of triumph, Sara slowly, almost deliberately, sauntered over towards the young goose. She seemed in no hurry to administer the kill. She was within two metres of the struggling gosling when a large gander landed on the grass in front of her. Sara stopped instantly, but she was too slow to avoid a series of swift pecks to her head. Yelping, she turned and ran for the safety of the house with the gander in close pursuit, its wings spread in offensive attack. I closed the door behind her and the enraged gander slammed into the glass. Sara peered out from behind my legs with an uncharacteristic 'who-me?' grin on her face.

The young gosling continued to struggle, but unable to free itself, it slumped over as if dead and I could see a band of bright red forming around its neck feathers just below its head where it was stuck in the wire.

My glorious smirk turned to one of horror. I stared at the fence for many moments aghast at what I saw. What a fool I had been. Was this gosling's life worth my grass? I thought not. After all, the main reason I came here was to commune with Nature and not to a city job I detested. How could I have been so selfish, so insensitive, I am the trespasser, not the geese. This is their home; they are not the uninvited squatter. I had to remind myself that I am only part of the greater scheme, not separate from it, like those city-dwellers. I had to learn to live with the other creatures of this planet, not against them. And here was my first lesson.

I ran down to the end of the yard hoping and praying I was not too late. Sara came too. She seemed to sense what had to be done and kept the gander busy while I tended to the gosling's needs.

I took its weight in my hand and parting the wire of the fence with my other hand, freed the young bird from its entanglement. I ran my fingers along its breast and under its wings checking for a heart-beat. It was some minutes before I could find an artery. The beat was strong and steady; a good sign. Looking down upon the fragile creature lying limp in my hand, I cursed my stupidity.

Back at the house I wrapped its wings and head in towels in case it should awaken on the drive to a local veterinary clinic.

For three days I fretted over the survival of the little gosling and questioned how I could have been so insensitive to the needs of this creature.

Finally, the veterinary hospital called. I returned to the clinic and brought the little goose home. I had never felt such a sense of belonging to this greater thing called Nature as I did at that moment. I hesitated reaping the rewards of a helping neighbour then set the young goose free just above the river. It waddled down the slight decline, clumsy and unsure, a little comical in its walk, but reaching the river it entered its rightful domain, all clumsiness gone. It swam out towards the lake like a ballet dancer skating across a stage. Three adult Canada geese swam out and escorted it back to the flock.

I stood for many moments in awe of such beautiful creatures and felt blessed that they shared some of their lives with me. I had already removed the fence and later that afternoon erected a sign that read, "Canada Geese Welcome. The Grass is Yours". And, in small print, "Be Aware of the Dog".

Toby's Meeting

The tree branch that grew across the front lawn was a favourite spot for Toby to lie, and he was there just lying in the sun, dreaming of lazy days, hamburgers, catnip, and his favourite person, his owner, the lady in the little house on the corner. He awoke with a start and sniffed the air. His ears were up and his whiskers out straight. He sniffed the air again and wondered what had awakened him, but everything seemed normal. Toby relaxed and yawned and began a stretch that started at the beginning of his black nose and ended in a slight shudder at the tip of his orange tail.

The wind blew and ruffled his fur and told him it was getting late. He leaped down from the branch and ran into the house. Now it was time for dinner. Later it would be time to think about the meeting he had called of all the cats in the neighbourhood.

Toby had just finished the last bit of food from his bowl when Tammy jumped from the window onto the porch. She leaned over and sharpened her claws on the wooden railing of the porch, her gentle eyes on Toby. "What's this thing you call a meeting all about tonight my hunt brother?"

Toby ignored her and began cleaning his whiskers.

Tammy stretched and yawned opening her mouth so wide it showed all her teeth.

Again Toby ignored her, but he kept one eye on her because she had a look on her face that said she was planning something mischievous.

"I'm so excited," continued Tammy. "I've never been to a meeting before. I'm not sure how to act or what to say? Can you tell me what a meeting is, and what it's for? What do we all do at the meeting?" Tammy waited a moment then gave a sneeze of laughter when Toby continued to ignore her and then leaped on him. They wrestled for a moment, batting each other with their paws in a play fight. Finally, tired out, they both lay back and began licking their fur preparing their coats for the meeting.

When Toby had finished his grooming he jumped away from the porch and bounded into the darkness heading for the back yard of the abandoned house next door where the meetings had always been held. "See you at the meeting," he shouted to Tammy who was still sitting on the porch. Tammy put one last patch of fur along her side straight then turned to follow Toby towards the neighbour's yard. Out from the house strolled Marty.

"Yesseree Bob! Off to the meeting I go.

No matter how fast, no matter how slow.

With the help of a friend, with the help of a foe,

We'll get there, that much I know.

But hurry we must, or be in the last row.

Tum, tum, dee dumm dum. Hee, hee, hee." Marty said. "Hurry along now, Tammy. I'm right behind you."

"You're weird, Marty, but you're okay. Come on then, let's go." So off to the meeting trotted Tammy followed closely by Marty, still singing his new song.

"Yesseree Bob! Off to the meeting we go.

No matter how fast, no matter how slow.

Tum, tum, dee dumm, dum."

When they arrived at the neighbour's house they walked around to the back yard to join all the cats from the neighbourhood. There must have been 25 cats all gathered for the meeting, including Tracy and Blue, most wondering what the meeting was all about because almost none of them had ever been to a meeting before. No one had called a meeting in the area for so long. In fact, no one could remember when the last meeting had been called. But most agreed a meeting was indeed a grand idea, but again no one ever had anything to talk about that needed a meeting to do it. Tammy and Marty took their places up near the front beside Tracy and Blue so they could hear better. "Oh, this is so exciting," said Tammy. "And there're ever so many cats here, some I have never seen before. I wonder where they all came from. I hope I look my best."

"Yesseree Bob," began Marty, the same way he began

almost every time he began something. "Very strange, very strange, so many cats all in one place, not natural, not natural, natural it is not."

"Don't know why I even bothered to come," stated Tracy. "I could be at home curled up on the rocking chair."

Toby was up at the front trying to get everyone's attention. "Aaahhhemm," Toby began, clearing his throat.

"This better be good," shouted Blue, not sure why he came either.

"Quiet everybody," shouted a white long-haired cat from the front row. "Let's hear what he has to say."

Finally, the high pitched murmur from the crowd of cats quieted to a low whisper and everyone waited for Toby to speak. They all wondered why this little orange cat had called a "meeting".

"Thank you all for coming to the meeting on such short notice," began Toby. "I called this meeting to discuss something of grave importance."

"What's grave importance mean, Tammy?" whispered Marty.

"It means it's really, really, really important, or you will go to your grave, I think."

"Oh, thank you," replied Marty. "You are so clever."

"Ssshhh, quiet, I can't hear," said a cat from behind. Marty turned and stuck out his tongue.

Toby continued, "And I wanted you all to hear it first hand, to get all the facts straight instead of hearing stories that may or may not be true." Toby paused for a moment to let all the cats think about what he just said then he continued. "Two dogs, a big black and orange boy dog and a light grey girl dog are on the loose on our streets and are terrorizing cats. Just a block south of here, two days ago, Blackie, an old black tom cat was chased by these dogs and he had to run up a tall tree to escape being attacked. His owner got a big red fire truck to come and it put a long thing up the tree and a man climbed up the thing and got him down. He had been up that tree all day before the big red truck came to get him down. And Cinder, a grey and white girl cat from around the corner has gone missing. She is not known to wander like many of us and it is feared she has been hurt and is now afraid to come home. And my litter mate, Marty," Toby pointed to Marty sitting in the front row.

This made Marty feel very important and he stood up tall on all four legs, lifted his nose in the air and pranced around in a circle so the other cats could see him better.

"He was cornered by the dogs yesterday and only got away when our owner came out of the house and frightened them away." The crowd of cats all began to talk amongst themselves.

"What are we going to do," shouted a new mother cat, her voice trembling. "I have a new litter of four kittens. How will I ever be able to protect them?"

"Come now," Toby shouted. "This is why I called the meeting so we could talk together and come up with a plan to make the neighbourhood safe again. Somehow we must get rid of these two dogs. They are both bigger than any one of us cats, and much stronger, but maybe if we face them in numbers we can make them understand we will not stand for any more of their foolishness."

There was much talking among all the cats. No one seemed to have any idea of what to do. And most were now very afraid. There was so much confusion it looked like the meeting was going to fall apart.

A big old striped grey tomcat came out of the crowd and turned and stood beside Toby at the front. "Ahemmm," he coughed so everyone would stop and pay attention to him. When everyone stopped talking, he began. "My name is Mulligan. It was very wise of this little orange cat," he stopped and turned to Toby. "What is your name son?"

"Toby."

"Yes, yes, thank you. Toby, to call this meeting," continued Mulligan. "There was a time when I was young, I would hate to say how long ago that was, that we had these meetings all the time.

Now we seem to be too busy grooming or sunbathing to be bothered with anyone else's troubles. But these dogs are a danger to all of us, and like," he stopped talking in the middle of the sentence and again turned towards Toby, whispering, "what is your name again, son?"

"Toby."

"Yes, Toby," Mulligan said in a whisper. Raising his voice again, he continued. "And like Toby said, if we are to rid the neighbourhood of these dogs, we must work together like we used to do in the old days."

"Hey, Mulligan you old fart!" yelled a cat from the back row. "So what do we do?"

"That is, uuummmmhh, just what I was coming to," sputtered Mulligan. "I think we should form a committee of five of our wisest cats and they should decide what to do. The committee will talk and then call another meeting to tell everyone what will be done. And I think this little orange cat should be on the committee. And I will also volunteer because I think I am probably the oldest cat here and probably the only cat who remembers what the old meetings were like, so we can conduct ourselves accordingly."

Everyone agreed! Three other cats were chosen: Jamie, a black and white tomcat because he was the biggest and strongest cat in the crowd, a second, Fluffy, a female because everyone thought a female should be on the committee, and the third was Marty because he knew what the dogs looked like.

"Yesssirreee Bob," said Marty. "I'm on the committee. Whoop it ee dee. Whoop it ee dee. What now, my little orange friend?"

"Well," said Toby, thinking. "I, I'm not sure. I guess we should wait until the crowd goes and then we five sit down and think of a plan to rid the neighbourhood of these dogs."

After everyone left, the five cats talked for many minutes, but no one could suggest anything that would get rid of the dogs because the dogs were so big and strong compared to even the largest of the cats.

Then Marty stood up. His eyes had turned all milky and

had that far away look he often got when it seemed he was in a trance and ready to speak words of wisdom. He spoke in a deep whisper that came from deep down in his tummy.

"Help is what we need,

Help we must get

To stop the bad deed

A trap we must set."

When Toby looked at Marty again, his eyes had returned to normal.

"Yesseree Bob," said Marty. "So what's the plan my little orange friend?"

Mulligan spoke next. "He is a strange cat, that one, but what he says is correct. We must set a trap for these dogs. So, come on lads, let's have your ideas."

The group of five cats spoke together for about another hour and still they could not come up with any ideas. They agreed they would think about it overnight and meet again the next day. But all agreed that it was necessary to decide quickly.

"If only we had a really big cat to frighten away the dogs," remarked Fluffy. "I saw a big orange one with black stripes the other day on that funny picture machine my owner always watches." Everyone agreed with her but no one knew where they could get such a big cat.

The next day the five cats again gathered in the meeting area. Of course Marty was late and Mulligan had already started when Marty arrived.

"Yeesssereee, Bob," said Marty, when he walked into the meeting area. "Must hurry, must hurry," he mumbled and walked up to Toby gave him a gentle swipe with his paw. "How are you my little litter mate? So nice to be included, it is it is."

"Well, lads," began Mulligan. "Are we are all here now?" He spoke as if he had taken over the meeting from Toby, but Toby didn't mind. Toby was at a total loss like everyone else about what to do. "Come on lads. Let's have your ideas." Mulligan asked again.

Not one of the cats could think what to do. After a few minutes of mumbling everyone was silent then Marty slowly pranced up to the front of the group and turned to face them. His eyes had turned milky again and had that far away look. He spoke!

"The dogs are too big,
The dogs are too strong.
A cat that's as big,
Does not belong.
It is only a toy,
And some stuffing is missing.
Hide inside is the ploy.
The cats growling and hissing.
It is there on the tables.
To the garage dark and gloomy,
With two cats to pull cables.
Doing this is the key.
A puppet you have made,
To the dogs it is frightening,
So the fear is repaid,
They will not be returning."

"That's it," said Toby. "I understand. Marty you are so clever."

Marty had returned to his normal self by this time and knew nothing of what Toby spoke. "What ever you say my little orange friend," he said and danced around in a little circle.

Now it was Mulligan's turn to be confused. "I don't understand. Can someone please tell me what's going on?"

"My owner has a big old stuffed toy cat on a table in my house with lots of dark brown fur around its head," said Toby. "What Marty suggested was to make a puppet from this big toy cat and use it to frighten the dogs away."

"I don't know," Mulligan hesitated.

"Do we have any other ideas?" asked Jamie.

No one had any other ideas so they decided to try it.

"We'll have to learn to growl really loud and low like I heard once on that box that shows pictures that my owner always watches," said Toby. "The big brown cats on that growled really loud."

Toby tried to growl the same, but couldn't get his voice down low enough. Then they all tried to growl like the lions Toby saw on television and only the big black and white cat, Jamie, came anywhere near sounding as ferocious. So it was decided that Jamie would be one of the two cats inside the stuffed lion. Strings attached to the lion's legs, tail and head would make it move and look like it was alive and angry.

"But, hey," said Mulligan. "Once we do all this, just how are we going to get the dogs to come to the garage?"

"I've been thinking about that," said Toby. "We'll get, my owner's dog, Nikkita, to find the dogs and talk them into coming to the garage to see the giant cat. When Nikkita tells them this cat is much bigger and stronger than them, they'll have to come and see for themselves."

The very next day, after the cats had rehearsed their giant cat act, Nikkita went looking for the two bad dogs. All the cats went to their appointed places in the little garage attached to the little house on the corner. Mulligan and Jamie crawled inside the stuffed lion toy, Toby and Tammy climbed up on the rafters of the garage to pull the strings attached to the stuffed lion and Blue and Tracy jumped up to the top of the shelves to throw paint cans down on the dogs when they came into the garage.

"You've got to be kidding," said the black and orange dog when Nikkita told him. "I don't believe that."

The light grey girl dog just laughed. "There isn't a cat in the world as big and as strong as us," she said.

"Well, if you don't believe me you will have come to the little garage at the side of the little house on the corner and I'll show you," argued Nikkita.

So the three dogs walked down the street to the little garage on the side of the little house on the corner.

"Now be careful," said Nikkita to the other two dogs when

they approached the garage. "It's there in the back corner, the dark back corner, and I think it's asleep."

The big black and orange dog entered the garage first and moved slowly towards the back corner with his nose out straight trying to smell the creature that was suppose to be in the corner. The light grey girl dog followed behind, also with her nose sniffing the air. They could smell cat, but couldn't see anything.

Jamie began his practised low growl.

The two dogs stopped dead in their tracks, their ears up and searched the shadows for what creature made that sound.

The two cats inside the stuffed lion, Mulligan and Jamie, got to their feet and Jamie growled again in as low a growl as he could make. Up on the rafters of the garage Toby and Tammy pulled the strings attached to the lion's head and paws. In the dark of the back corner the creature really looked like a giant cat getting to its feet. Mulligan, inside at the back end of the lion, tried to follow Jamie's paw-steps, but he tripped on Jamie's tail and stumbled against the shelves. Tracy and Blue and four empty paint tins sitting on top of the shelves all fell to the floor just as Jamie and Mulligan jumped towards the two dogs. All four cats were snarling and growling especially Mulligan when one of the paint tins fell on his head.

At the sight of this giant cat coming towards them snarling and growling like something from the deepest jungle and throwing paint tins and little cats as well, the two dogs turned with their tails between their legs and ran yelping up the street.

None of the cats could stop laughing at the sight of these two big dogs running away like puppies scared of the unknown. Just for good measure all the cats together let out a big roar.

Marty, watching it all from the safety of the tree branch, shouted after the dogs, "Yeeesssereee Bob. And don't come back, **ever**."

And the dogs never did. Once again peace settled into the cat community around the little house on the corner.

Marty is in the foreground, Toby is eating out of the food dish with Tammy behind.

§

Tracy's Gift

Ho, ho, ho, I heard a jolly fat man say,
In his suit of red and reindeer sleigh.
He came down the chimney on a wintry night,
And made so much noise it gave me a fright.

Just who or what I did not know,
But from out of the soot came a merry ho, ho.
Stepping into the light I could see the sack
Brimming with gifts slug over his back.

He worked quickly now with nary a care,
Filling the stockings hanging there by the chair.
Gift after gift he placed by the tree,
And drank the milk I thought was for me.

Meooow", I complained in my little voice,
But he was bigger than me so I had no choice.
With nary a sound he hurried now,
Ignoring me and my little meow.

Gobbling down the cookie snack,
Over his shoulder he threw his sack.
His job now done, he turned to leave,
Wiping his whiskers across his sleeve.

Pausing a moment he turned to me.
And smiled and whispered, Merry Christmas Tracy.
With the wave of a hand and another ho, ho,
Up the chimney again he did go.

But in his haste to be on his way,
Perhaps forgotten there on the tray.
I found some milk and a big cookieee,
That indeed he left as a gift for meee.

JOHN FORREST

JOHN retired after 34 years as an educator and began writing about the exceptional events and wonderful people that have enriched his life. Drawing on these experiences, he strives to recreate the emotion and impact of those special moments in life that touch us all.

His short stories have be published in the magazines, *Reminisce* and *Good Old Days, Capper's, New Moon Network,* the syndicated newspaper feature, *The Front Porch* and in Lake Simcoe Living. Annually, since 2001 The Orillia Packet and Times has published his Christmas stories in a serialized format. John's stories have appeared in the anthologies; *Chicken Soup for the Soul (Christmas 2007, Fathers and Sons 2008, True Love 2009* and *Oh Canada 2011), My Teacher Is My Hero 2008), A Cup of Comfort For Inspiration (2003)* and *For A Better World 2010), Our Literary Lapses 2009* and *From The Cottage Porch 2011.* John's works have also aired on CBC Radio One's *First Person Singular* and won first place in competitions held by; *The Toronto Sun, The Orillia Packet and Times and The Owen Sound Sun Times.* His book: *"Angels Stars and Trees - Tales of Christmas Magic" (Your Scrivener Press 2007),* an anthology of Christmas stories, was released to excellent reviews and the second edition has sold out. Current projects include a second Christmas anthology and a humour anthology

John is a founding facilitator with the Mariposa Writers' Group and of that group's annual Lake Country Literary Lapses Festival. He lives in Severn Township near Orillia, Ontario, with his wife Carol, where they enjoy golf, travel and following the life adventures of their grown children Rob and Dana.

Dad's Dinghy!

The rich fabric of a family's history can be woven from the most modest of materials and the relationship between a father and son can be strengthened in surprising ways. Such was the case one cottage summer of my youth, when I built Dad's dinghy.

Friends of our family had a cottage and a small cabin on Sand Lake near Kearney, just north of Huntsville, Ontario. For six glorious summers in the late nineteen fifties and early sixties, my mother, my little brother Will and I travelled north, took up residence in the cabin and spent July and August on vacation. In return, we were responsible for the upkeep of the property and the big cottage. There were lots of chores to do, but when you're 11 years old, splitting firewood, carrying water from the spring and even liming "the outhouse" was more like fun than work. Dad worked in Toronto, but each weekend he would make the 400 mile round trip to visit us.

The time I looked forward to most was the last two weeks of August, when Dad's plant would shut down and he would join us for a family vacation. This year's holiday was to be particularly special because he would be bringing a small sailboat with him. During WW II, while stationed in England, Dad had fallen in love with sailing. Following his return from the war, feeding and housing his family took precedence over recreational activities; but this year he was scheduled to receive a vacation bonus and it had been earmarked for the purchase of a used sailboat.

As I recall it was only about ten feet long. The sail had grayed, the ropes were frayed and much of the varnish had bubbled; but to Dad it was a yacht. I was eagerly looking forward to crewing for Dad and spending hours together flying across the waters of Sand Lake on white canvas wings. Then disaster struck.

The week before his holiday, Dad sent a telegram to say that his bonus had been deferred until Christmas. This would be another summer without sails.

That night, as I lay in my bed mulling things over, I had

115

an idea for a substitution and as my eyelids grew heavy with sleep, I remember thinking that I had just five days to work on it.

Early the next morning I got busy. Fortunately, I already had access to the most basic requirement; a boat. Dragged up on shore was an ancient, flat-bottomed skiff that served as a work-boat. It was a weather beaten gray in colour and badly in need of minor repairs; but it seated two (three in a pinch) and leaked only a little. It would do! Next I needed a sail. I talked Mum into donating a large flowered oilcloth that had seen better days as a picnic table cover. Now what could I use for a mast?

One of my summer jobs had been to clear out a section of brush near the big cottage. Some of the saplings that had fallen victim to my axe now came in handy as my mast and spars. I built a rectangular framework and then stretched the oilcloth over it, nailing it into place with about a pound of those big-headed gray shingle nails. Next I had to marry the sail and the boat or, as I learned later in life, step the mast.

Splitting hardwood ends from the local sawmill into firewood for the cook stoves and Quebec heaters, was another of my cottage chores. I searched through the woodpile for one that would wedge between the middle seat and the thwart of the work-boat and used its rotting hollow centre as a snug holder for the butt of the mast. After scrounging an old paddle from one of the canoes to act as a rudder; I was ready to try my creation. I had intended to use my seven year-old brother Will as crew, but Mum vetoed that. Instead, she offered to accompany me on the maiden voyage of what I had decided should be christened Dad's Dinghy. The prevailing wind on Sand Lake was always on-shore during the day making sailing away from land, with this craft, impossible. So, Mum spun the sail sideways to prevent it catching the wind and I strained mightily at the oars rowing us far enough from shore to gain some maneuvering room. Once we were in position, I took up my paddle rudder and signaled Mum to turn the mast.

The wind caught our square sail, billowing the oilcloth and we began to glide silently across the surface of the lake. As we picked up speed the water began burbling at the bow and we actually left a small wake as we raced the waves toward shore.

I held us on course but Mum was hard pressed to keep the sail square to the wind and she hung on grimly as we charged toward land. With her back to the bow Mum couldn't see where we were going and I was so excited at the success of my invention, I forgot to warn her to turn the sail. Not only did we reach shore, we ran right up onto to the beach, coming to a sudden stop as the bow of our craft crunched into the sand. Mum was thrown off balance and lost her grip on the sail, which promptly spun into the wind, cracking me on the side of the head with the lower spar. An ignominious end! But no matter; we had survived the first voyage of Dad's Dinghy.

Mum and Will and I spent the rest of that week making modifications and taking shakedown cruises. We added some rigging and discovered that by using the oars as out-riggers, we could even make a little headway across the wind. Dad's Dinghy wasn't showy, but she sailed and by Friday night she was ready for her namesake's vacation. I wanted to surprise Dad, so I took the boat around the point about a mile away and tied it to a friend's dock.

I was asleep when Dad arrived later that night; but I was up and away early the next morning to watch for my chance. After breakfast, Dad would always take his second cup of coffee down to the beach where he would sit in one of the big wooden Muskoka chairs and gaze out over the lake. That was my cue. I rowed out from behind the point.

The light morning breeze was just right, so I set sail and laid course for the spot where Dad was sitting. I'm not sure what Dad thought when he first spotted this strange craft drifting toward him, but he did sit up and take notice.

As I approached shore I'm certain he recognized the old gray boat and the flowered tablecloth sail; but he couldn't see me until the bow crunched into the sand near him.

"Ahoy!" I said, "Would you like to go for a sail?"

I can still picture the smile on Dad's face as he studied the design of that very unique craft. No son, and I suspect no father, could have been prouder than we were that morning.

Dad took over as Captain while Will and I acted as crew. We sailed every day of his vacation, learning the ropes and making modifications that rendered Dad's Dinghy even more seaworthy. It was a wonderful two weeks!

But eventually, like all good things, our summer of sailing came to an end. On that last Saturday night we had a bonfire on the beach and toasted marshmallows on long sticks. The sun had set, the night air became cool and the warmth rising from the waters of the lake created a gentle offshore breeze. It was a perfect night for a sail. I took Will up to the cabin and stayed to baby-sit, while Dad escorted Mum to the boat.

The last time I saw Dad's Dinghy it was slipping silently away from shore, following a path of rippling moonlight across the limpid waters of Sand Lake.

Next morning the oilcloth sail was covering the woodpile and the old gray skiff was pulled well up on shore and turned over for the winter. Summer was over.

Dad eventually got his sailboat and together we spent many happy hours on the waters of Sand Lake. But the memory of Dad's Dinghy, and the family bond that special home-made craft helped forge, lingers still.

One of Those Mornings

The irritating buzz of the alarm dragged me from my dreams and I reached out from beneath the covers to silence it. My fumbling fingers found the snooze button, pressed and then recoiled in shock at the feel of the frigid plastic. " Oh no," I groaned, "not again!"

Rolling on to my side I hauled the covers higher on my shoulder, pressed up against my wife Carol and kissed her awake. The radio clicked on and 1570 CFOR's morning man, Rusty Draper, confirmed my fear. Overnight, the temperature in Orillia had plummeted to a record 30 degrees below zero. I knew for certain that this would be ... *one of those mornings.*

It was early March 1973 and I was teaching a grade 4/5 class at Orillia's Mount Slaven Public School. I had accepted the job in the Fall and was to begin in January. Although we were eager to move to the heart of Ontario's "cottage country", like most young couples Carol and I were long on ambition and short on cash. However, we had managed to scrape together a down payment and over Christmas Break, we abandoned our comfortable city apartment and took up residence in an old summer cottage on the eastern shore of Lake Couchiching. Although idyllic in the summer, our new home was isolated and ill-suited to winter occupancy. We had managed to install a toilet, water-heater and a bathtub but the conditions were still spartan. An acorn fireplace and temperamental old oil stove were our only sources of heat and there was no insulation, so frozen pipes and drains were a common and frustrating occurrence in our frigid abode. But, we prided ourselves on our ability to cope. Outfitted in arctic boots and snowsuits; we spent that first winter shovelling tons of snow, splitting cords of wood and using a blow dryer to thaw our frozen plumbing. We battled the elements, coming to grips daily with the rigors of rural living. However, it seemed that this morning would provide us with our toughest test yet.

We had awakened in a freezer! The minus 30 temperature had jellied the stove oil, cutting the flow of fuel to the space heater and I knew our water lines would be frozen. It would have been a perfect day to stay in bed; however, as a probationary teacher, I just had to get to school.

I tested the temperature with a puff of breath over the edge of the bedspread, and watched in horror as a vapour cloud rose toward the ceiling. Bracing myself, I flipped the covers off and leaped to the floor. The icy cold of the linoleum seared my naked feet as, like a novice firewalker, I danced my way down the hallway to the heater. I opened the reserve tank, struck a match and thankfully the flame caught.

Fortunately the pipes in the bathroom had not split and after some carefully applied heat from the blow dryer, hot water steamed from the bathtub spout. As I settled thankfully into the wonderful warmth of the water, I heard a thumping sound from the front room.

Carol had risen to begin her chores. After thawing the kitchen taps she left them running to flush the system and began using her trusty hatchet to split kindling for the fireplace. "What a team!" I thought, as I lay in the bath; unaware of the drama unfolding in the kitchen.

You see, although the taps had thawed, the drain was still frozen. The water running in was not running out. The sink overflowed and water began splashing onto the super-cooled surface of the linoleum floor. Distracted, Carol turned her attention away from her task, just as the hatchet was descending. Her shriek of pain split the arctic air.

Galvanized, I leaped from the tub, water streaming from my body as I rushed to her rescue. When I reached the front room, I was confronted by a grisly scene.

My mate was seated in front of the fire place, left hand clutched in her right; blood seeping from between her fingers and dripping on to the hearth.

She was crying, "I cut my finger off!" "I cut my finger off!"

With my attention focused on Carol, I failed to spot the danger awaiting me and stepped, naked and unprepared, firmly onto the slick icy floor of the kitchen.

My feet flew out from underneath me; I crashed down butt first in the slush, slid wildly across the room and slammed into the wall. By the time my head cleared Carol was alternating between sobbing in pain and laughing at me.

Still, it was obvious that swift medical attention was needed. Carol was already dressed, so I wrapped her hand in a makeshift tea towel bandage and hastily donned my own snowmobile suit for the trip to town. Thankfully, the block heater had kept our faithful Chevy warm enough to start. However the rest of the vehicle including the heater was frozen solid. No problem! With me driving and Carol wielding a window scraper in her uninjured hand; we pounded on flat-spotted tires, along Rama Road to Soldiers' Memorial Hospital.

The nurse in Emergency escorted Carol directly in for treatment, leaving me to handle the paperwork. Needing my wallet, I reached up grabbed the zipper on my skidoo-suit and pulled; opening it to my navel. "Oops!" I was naked underneath.

While the receptionist and I turned matching shades of red, I hastily re-zipped and provided from memory, what information I could. A doctor invited me into the treatment room. Carol had been very lucky! Although she would suffer a permanent loss of feeling in the tip of her finger, the bone was undamaged and her nail and much of the severed flesh would grow back! Some stitches, a bandage and sling and after a call to my very understanding Principal, we headed home.

Once there I carefully rekindled the fireplace and made coffee. As Carol and I sat quietly in the glow of the fire, looking at each other over the rims of our steaming mugs, subtle smiles spread slowly across our faces. Although bruised and bloodied; we raised our cups and sipped, silently congratulating ourselves on surviving; *one of those mornings.*

The Coach

I was taping a motivational phrase to my son's bedroom mirror, when the memories came flooding back …

The final horn sounded in my mind. The bench cleared en-masse and the on-ice celebration began. We were winners; but it was the end. As a team, we would never play another game.

Order was being restored when I spotted the tall figure standing alone at the gate of our players' box. I knew he would not join us on the rink. Retrieving the game puck from the melee, I skated toward him and proffered it.

His name was Frank Danby, but to me he was simply, "The Coach".

The Coach took on the task of forming a new ice-hockey team, out of a group of teenagers that was literally a 1950's version of Disney's Mighty Ducks. We were not his first hockey team, but we would be his last. Most of us were local guys, new to the league and a number were cast-offs, cut from teams in neighbouring communities. We had a wide range of size, talent and personalities, some very good players and a lot of other boys who wanted to be. From scorers to checkers we would become The Coach's team, and no one who gave their best was ever cut or benched to help us win.

Ice time was scarce in those days and older teams drew the worst practice times. Ours was brutal; Saturday Mornings, at 6:30 a.m.. We whined. The Coach responded by convincing the arena's manager to let us on earlier and challenged us to skate with him, starting at 5:30 a.m.! Although he was in his sixties, The Coach was always first on the ice; and even though some of us arrived a little worse for wear, straight from Friday night dates and parties; no one even considered skipping one of those two-hour practices.

I can still feel the frigid arena air, grabbing at my lungs as we skated our warm-up circuits. The snick, snick of skate blades carving fresh ice was music to our ears. It was a time before helmets and as we ran our drills the heat rose from our heads, forming vaporous halos in the freezing air above. Gliding, bent at the waist, sticks across our knees, sucking wind; we sprang back into action at each blast of his whistle. We would skate, shoot and check to the point of exhaustion and then beg to be allowed to scrimmage for the pure joy of it.

And when it was over, we suffered the delicious agony of tingling toes when the skates came off and warmth began to seep slowly back into numbed feet.

Every Saturday, The Coach was there, teaching and guiding as he put us through our paces. He honed and made the most of what skills we possessed and he set an example for us in his attitude toward sport. For him, winning wasn't everything, nor the only thing; how you played the game was!

I can see him still; a tall, gaunt, figure stooped slightly at the shoulders, towering above us behind the players' bench; fedora pushed slightly up on his forehead. His demeanour was calm and his expression was thoughtful and all knowing. His voice was low and gravelly and he spoke in measured tones, with the odd "humph" for emphasis. He rarely yelled and I can't remember him ever berating a player.

The Coach didn't demand respect; he commanded it! You knew that if you practised and played his way; hard, clean and smart and gave a hundred percent every time you laced up your skates, the winning would take care of itself. It did, and we became a force to be reckoned with.

Two years in a row we made the finals, but two years in a row injury forced me to sit in the stands and watch in frustration as teams with perhaps more individual talent, but certainly less character, denied us the goal we sought. Some coaches might have cut me, or others, and found new players; or bemoaning their fate called it quits; but not The Coach. He knew it was just a matter of a little more time and assured us our time would come. It had.

Next year came and we never lost again. Two years, undefeated over 90 games, two League Pennants, two County Titles and a City Championship. Nobody beat The Coach's team, ever again. We couldn't have known then the pride he felt, but I understand now. Pride, not just in winning, but in moulding a bunch of boys into a team of young men. The Coach taught us more than hockey skills; he taught us skills for life. And as the years passed, he followed the careers of his boys and spoke often, with pride, of their success in business, education and sport.

Today I'm a coach and my son plays hockey. The verse I was taping to his mirror was a mantra shared with us by The Coach; a quote from sportswriter Grantland Rice.

It read: "When the one great scorer comes, to mark against your name; it matters not who won or lost, but how you played the game."

As I smoothed the last piece of tape to the mirrored glass, my reminiscence ended ...

The Coach took the puck from my hand. Tough teenage defencemen aren't supposed to cry; so no words were exchanged. He studied it for a moment turning it slowly in his hand. That battle-scarred black disc represented the achievement of a dream and the end of a four-year journey, which would forever mark the lives of a dozen young men. The Coach looked me in the eye and nodded, then slipped it into the pocket of his coat, turned and walked slowly down the ramp toward the locker room.

Not much of a trophy; but it was enough.

The Coach is on the exteme left of the middle row.
I (John) am the tallest player in the middle row.

The Show Must Go On

In the 1930s, my father was one of a group of neighbourhood children, which performed an annual summer show. Twenty-five years later that experience and his wisdom would touch my life.

Each year, one family on Beresford Street in Toronto would designate its backyard as that year's "Theatre". A "fairytale" script was always selected, roles would be assigned and under the watchful eyes of a half a dozen block mothers, practices would begin. Children were recruited from every family on the block and everyone capable had a role; no matter how small. Bashful boys came out of their shells and giggly girls became sophisticated starlets, as lines were learned and scenes were blocked. However, it seemed that every production involved some sort of embrace and often a dreaded kiss by the leading actors.

One year, my then 10-year-old father was cast in the role of Prince Charming. He was less than enthusiastic about the part, the "frilly" costume he had to wear and the intimate scene he had to play with Sleeping Beauty. But of course the show had to go on and even the most reluctant and timid children were expected to rise to the occasion.

The presentation of the play was reserved for the last Saturday in August, when the chosen backyard would be transformed. The "wings" were blankets suspended from convenient clotheslines; the scenery was painted on sheets and hung from the back fence; the stage was a carpet covered lawn and the costumes and props were home-made. Lawn chairs and garden benches, of every description, were collected and assembled to provide comfortable seating for the expected large audience of parents, grandparents, other relatives and friends.

There were only two performances; a matinee for the mothers and their friends and an evening performance for the men-folk, most of whom still worked a six-day week. Both performances invariably brought down the house. The final bows of the evening were always accompanied by enthusiastic applause and followed by refreshments.

Out would come a large tub of ice, filled with green glass bottles of Coke for the actors and ice cream treats would follow. For

the men, foamy mugs of beer flowed from a keg, while pitchers of both plain and "special" iced tea were available for the more genteel members of the audience. And of course for all, a large frosted cake decorated with the name and year of the play.

As the evening wore on, each and every child's performance received critical acclaim and predictions of stardom on stage or screen, were made for most. Little did the audience or the actors know that, in less than ten years, many of the children in those shows would be at war; fighting in Europe and the Pacific, or working in factories in support of our Armed Forces. Some of them would not return. Thankfully my father did.

Well what goes around comes around. It came to pass that, when I was 9 years old, I was cast as the leading Tin Soldier in our school's Christmas Pageant. I hated my "silly" costume and having to sing a solo, on bended knee, to my female co-star had me suffering from acute embarrassment and severe "stage fright". I was refusing to go

through with it. Then Dad intervened. He dug two pictures out of the family archives and told me the stories behind each. One, was a group shot of The Beresford Street Players, Cast of Sleeping Beauty (circa 1933), with himself at age 10, seated cross-legged in the front

126

row, resplendent in his Prince Charming costume and flanked by his adoring Princess co-stars.

The other photo had been taken just 9 years later. It showed him as a 19 year old "tail gunner", in full flying gear, posed with his crew beside the Lancaster bomber that would during WW II, carry them safely through many perilous missions over enemy territory.

We talked about fear and what made us afraid. He didn't try to persuade me or tell me what to do. But as he described why and how he had faced those two very different but similar challenges; I began to understand the importance of duty, commitment and not letting others down. His final statement did the trick. Even then, I was old enough to understand the wry humour in his admission that;

"John, as I recall, I was probably more afraid of having to kiss Sleeping Beauty; than I ever was of flying through enemy flak and fighters!"

The show must go on and thanks to a father's wisdom, understanding and support; I did, too!

WILLIAM J. GIBSON

BILL was born in St. Catherines, Ontario in 1953.

He graduated from the University of St. Michael's College at the University of Toronto where he studied Modern Poetry with Professor Marshall McLuhan.

He also has a Teaching and Training Adults Certificate from Georgian College. Bill was a technical writing consultant for 25 years with clients including Amex Canada, IBM Toronto Lab, Canada Wire and Cable, Ontario Ministry of Education, Ontario Ministry of Community and Social Services, Clearnet, Cyberplex, The Writing Factory, Unitel, Toyota Credit Canada, and the Huronia Museum.

In the 1990s, Bill and Denis Stokes established Alburnum Press, a small literary press specializing in poetry chapbooks. He lives in Victoria Harbour, Ontario. His favourite poem is the book-long *Paterson* by William Carlos Williams.

At Cat Island, South Carolina 2002

by the tidewater channel
between two islands
I sat on the pier bench
watching the water
watching the light
on the water

the dolphins rose
and rolled over
breaking the surface
shining grey curls
hunting for dinner
in the turning tide

I listened to them
taking their breath
and off to the west
Marines training
on Parris Island
fired mortars
and machine guns

the sky was grey
trying to be blue
a pelican and egret
showed the white side
of the morning

four vultures soared
over the darkened trees
black wings in the
changed sky

Heard Something in Your Voice

heard something in your voice
on the phone
a bit of alligator, no
a frantic anteater, no
your mother's attitude to responsibility
no not that either

you were in orbit with John Glenn
nope
your bad hair day had made you shave your head
no

then I remembered the last time you
sounded like this

I remember how you
said something
about the space race
the need for space, the
nature of relationships
ski poles
24 valve engines
black and white discernment in every
moment of a colour blown day
personal negative buoyancy
about limits and fig
newtons, the parabola
of confusion
sipping a glass of St. Emilion
no, that was another night
you had heard John Prine one time too little
I was Steve McQueen
you were Joan of Arc, no
I was Winchester on MASH, no
you were returning overdue library books, no

the snow kept falling like in a movie
we were not cold
we were in bed, no
we were driving somewhere, not talking
no, talking, no arguing, no ending it, no
we were happy, no
the garage door rose up
no
it was nothing, I imagined the whole thing

you and your voice should sit down
and work this out
a little sub committee

what did you say

§

Love Poem Number One

The softest skin, yours,
The grin you hurl at me over your strong shoulder,
You pump the pedals of your bicycle,
That grin flies back
Faster than your laugh,
Twenty miles an hour slower than your happy chatter

The best laugh, yours,
Makes my legs tighten
And I strain to catch every second
With you and the next and the next.
It all tumbles over me
Like warm rain
Before midnight and sleep a long way away.

The golden hair, yours,

Warms my arm,
Holds my heart up from the dark,

We gentle each other,
Speaking softly
Hearing our sounds and their words
And the ease that gathers us in is ours

For as long
As we can feel the laughter in the rain.

§

Love Poem Number Two

smile brightens and shines
the short string of words
fired like a happy burst of laughter
"My God, you can talk fast."

I remember sitting with you
beside the pool in Florida
with the pocket of kids
splashing in the shallow end

I asked you if you wanted kids
and you didn't answer for a moment
I studied your face
your eyes hidden behind
the pink framed sunglasses
wondering what your answer might be
wondering if you would answer

then you spoke slowly
"Yes, I want to have kids. Two boys."

the palm tree overhead nodded in agreement

I could hear the traffic on A1A behind us
the kids splashed and splashed and splashed
and you turned to look at me and smiled

So I sat quietly wondering if it would be me
who'd share two cowboys with you
because I know the man will be happy
and the cowboys will be luckier than they know

that evening we ate lobster again
and drove around the streets of Boca Raton
and admired all the quiet homes on the canals
and I wondered how many small cowboys
were dreaming behind the darkened windows.

§

Red Jack on a Red Queen

Hope is such a small step. You understand.
One more stone forward in a garden. Walking.

If the sun invites the shadows
to hide, the air to slip over
the flowers, then we are blinded.

We cannot see the blooms
end in October. The squirrel is only
running ahead of winter. Knowing.

The heavy, dark weight of snow,
all the wrong colour, not even

the temperature of hell, but I suspect
the same constant state.

Waiting time, dark time, winding

the clock does not assist,

not an aid to escape. You told me that once.
You told me that I knew this before. Remembering the simple
patterns, my choice of changes and persistence.

The stubbornness of love, the confusion of care
for caring. The reflex knows the hammer.

The doctor in a lab coat, the room like no other.
Surrendering the pilot wheel for a moment.

Becoming a pirate again, the comfort of that.
I do not know the end of the sea.

You are you, I am the person I always was.
The rubber nose, eyebrows and glasses have failed.

This is just a string of words and words. Naming it
in a puzzle is not being. What

the heart handles, the mind camouflages
imperfectly. It is a smooth stone turned over and over.
A game acquired after childhood.

I remember what my mother made me for lunch
on the day I broke my arm. The rain
coming pushes that button for me, over and over.
Baked apples after ham sandwiches and milk.

You are not here. I am where I usually am.
Running words through a cipher machine

and calling it understanding myself and
being grown up and being true. The old

familiar twist of surprise, catching myself
cheating at Solitaire. Red Jack on a Red Queen.

The radio crackles like bacon too long on the heat.

The storm comes. The shadows grow fast.
They do not need to be sure. They hold the garden.

The garden will not run away. The garden.

§

Care 1979

67, then 89, then 112, and 72, 75,
The oscilloscope shows the light green
Scratch of his heart beat.
The monitor is above his head,
On a special shelf, turned around
So he can't see it from his bed.
I sit here inside
The two curtained glass wall
And the open doorway of his room,
Which isn't really a room at all,
The nursing station a few feet
Behind me in the centre of this unit,
The glass walls wrapped
In a ring around the station.

"I was reading about Canadiens in The Star," he says.
I nod my head.
"They're in a bad slump, Dad.
It hasn't been the same since Dryden."
"Maybe it was him," he says.

He says his words
In a strange slack way.
His chest didn't explode.
There was a little pop,
A warning bell,

And he came in here to find out
What his body was muttering about.

But he's piled on twenty years over the nights.
He looks like someone I never saw. before.
He's scared and a little confused
And hating the place, and his body
That's betrayed him.
And he never thought about death before,
Not like he's thinking about it now.
He isn't saying any of this in words.
I'm watching his hands
And the corners of his mouth,
And his eyes.

His pulse rate per minute,
The green number, winks, changing every second or so.
98, 110, then 73, and I keep the corner of my eye there
And watch the strange wiggle
Of his heart arrhythmia on the oscilloscope.
He told me that nurses
Have come running in
To ask him how he feels
When the rhythm scatters,
Green lines scratching
In a mad tangle on the glass circle
And the paper strips of the monitor in their station,
And he looked up from his magazine
And said, "Fine.... Why?" And they went back.

79, 84, 112, 78, 97, 93, 56, 57,
Winking green numbers
Plucking at my eyes.
"I think they'll take the Cup this year.
But I don't know how long it will last."
"... with Pollock gone," I finish.
We nod together two sages of sports,

Ready to hammer out the column
When Dunnell packs it in.
No trouble at all.

Talking normal words in this fish bowl.
Stepping around in this conversational minuet.

Twenty feet down the open hall,
The monitor alarm triggered,
The long wail of the machine,
And I slide my eyes
To the doctor, the nurses,
And the crash cart, moving fast.
"Lafleur isn't right. Four games without a point."
I hear the sound of the electric paddles.
Just like on TV.
"He'll turn it around.
The defense are losing the games
For them," I say.

97, then 59, 112,
Then 105, 99, 130, 94, 64, 68,
The green scratch is settled and regular. The half frame reading glasses
On the tip of his nose.

His eyes push toward my face.
I check.

My feet are on the ends of my legs, And I am sitting In the chair,
The way chairs are sat In,
Andy my hands are relaxed
Stuck In the pockets of my jeans.

98, then 92, I am behaving super-normally
Leaving the crying to him
When Mom visits, and to my sister most of the time.
93, 112, 68, they've gone back to the station.

They've got the guy's heart restarted.
"That's the third time today," he says.

94 winks down to me.
Pushes at my face.
It feels like there's a hot needle
Scratching his heart beat into my face.

§

Dutchie Goes Down the Road 1974

The little Dutch boys played
around the bunker,
threw hand grenades and fired
the Schmeisser Machine Pistols,
Live ammunition for toys
after the death of the war
in the spring and summer of '45.
They were half starved kids
but they had the strength to play.
They could run where they wanted
except for the minefields,
of course.

Dutchie told me about it
after beating my ass for the second time
at chess, in the rec hall, at Syncrude
north of Fort McMurray, Alberta
"We had everything we wanted.
It was just lying around," he laughed.
He stayed in camp that weekend
so he wouldn't drink, he was tired of it.

He had a house in Red Deer.

The morning they let him go
he was drunk.
The General Foreman was an old pal of his.
But it didn't matter.

His back hoe stuck in the muskeg mud.
He'd walked it off his log pads.
His thermos bottle had been full of vodka.
"I don't give a shit," he said.

They used the widepad D5 cat
to come in and hook up the tow cable.
That cat could practically float on water
with those extra wide tracks.
The mud was so glue-like,
held the hoe tight, so stubborn
that the cable snapped
and the General Foreman
got missed by the flying cable
by about six feet or so
He would have been cut in half.
A little like a Schmeisser
might have chopped him.

My operator swore.
Then he laughed,
"Boy, that'll sure ruin your day."
Everyone who was there witnessing the event
took a step or two back.
I took more than that.

Dutchie laughed and laughed.
"Screw it," he said.
His great potatohead face
with the skull-close crew cut
and his big flapping ears,
he had no chest but a decent beer gut,
white reedy arms.
He looked past all of us.
He was already down the road
driving south to Red Deer
where he owned two houses.

That was home.

Someone took the crewcab
to get another tow cable.
A thicker one.

Dutchie threw his thermos bottle
as far as he could,
the orange and tan vessel
arcing out
over the torn up mud, clay and muskeg.
He stepped into the cab of the hoe,
slammed the door shut.
We could hear his portable radio start up.
A country tune.

"Leave him alone,"
said the General Foreman.
"We need to get another hoe in here.
He's not going anywhere."

§

In the Bar

we stand behind our high chairs at the bar
     like matadors ready for something new
the women come in & go out
     or wait   they watch   we look
our conversation about them
     or not rating losing all ability to think
     derailed when one beauty
or another walks past
     we drink too much   it is almost enough
the game is on the TV
     suspended 15 feet above our heads.
you have a toy bet with one of the waiters
     just for $25   a sliver of distraction
beyond the glass wall the taxis slide north
     the snow falling harder   in diagonal stripes.
"another day in paradise" you say, and then
     "you have to share the love."
I think about the meaning of something
     as I always do and remember what I said before
"everyone in their mind is eighteen forever
     no matter what lies our bodies tell us."

I remember when we were young
        and knew better   at least we thought we did.
then you start talking about God
        and eternity   then take out your cell phone
to see the number of your latest call
        and I start to laugh because we are not killing time
we are out playing   drinking   talking   smoking
        laughing   being a little stupid & more bitter
than the lemon   on the asshole's bottle of Corona
        standing next to me   who keeps asking me about golf.
I look past to last week & the young blonde
        we talked with in here   & her girlfriend who was going
to New York City to act & wasn't pretty enough
        but the blonde was   & when she slipped off her
black leather suit jacket   my eyes fell on her bare
        shoulders   her twenty-four-year-old honey skin
that led past the gold chain & locket
        to the tops of her breasts   & she laughed
& *it was summer & I was over there*
        & had   been swimming for a long time & my muscles
my back   & legs
        & arms hummed   quietly
        over & over again   the same curved line
the pure curved line
        in the sun   that was nothing
        not magic   not thought   not any damned thing
my body tired with the sweet
        tired of play   without
        my mind turning   over the pieces of the mechanism
like the old watchmaker I have become
        never dreamed I
        would go directly there   my life
and I knew absolutely that my lips would
never slide to the nape of her neck
and only the last thought was in her head too
she drank dry martinis until   the guy showed up
she had been waiting for   who ignored us politely
he was dressed exactly   like a magazine advertisement
the ink still wet   she talked to two other guys
to keep him   in the right state of balance
we watched him panting for her for an hour
        he hid it brilliantly & they left
for a party or something   you drank scotch   doubles

I switched back to beer   you won the bet in overtime.
at last   my taxi driver & I did not speak   about God.
        the snow fell harder & harder   making
the streetlights & the Christmas lights
very very pretty.

§

Stanley Park Zoo

The cases for the snakes looked small to me.
Some of the snakes were big. Very big.
The monkeys looked cold in the evening air.

The sidewalk art salesman told me
the river otters only worked for a big crowd.
I had come to see them three times
and failed to get a glimpse.
The polar bears were sleeping.
I stared at those enormous paws
moving lightly as they dreamed.

The geese, ravens, ducks, and pigeons
wandered everywhere working
the crowd for handouts.
The trees were so wonderfully tall.
The flowers hurt my eyes.
But I didn't cry.

I watched the little kids
totter after the geese,
the birds accelerated like Rolls Royces
over the close cropped lawn
leaving the kids with bread in their hands
wondering what to do next.

The Idea of Order on Langton Ave

We were talking about clutter.
How the hell to get a handle on
      the swamp of papers and files,

boxes of hurry, the need for some
      secret method to make it all
      perfect, when I saw the photo

you had shown me before,
      your face between your mother's
      and your father's at the dinner

for their anniversary, all the smiles,
but a different look in your eyes
      or maybe I just add that after

you told me that the doctors
      lost you on the table that morning
      for a short while and how you

knew you could go on to
      the other side, but you weren't
      ready, there was more here for you.

much more than heaps of paper
much more than me
but that was ten years before me.

And puzzles and projects and
fixing things all appeal to my brain
which my body carries around for me

So I offered the only thought that has
ever made sense to me about
      the idea of order.

"You have to decide the place
where things will go.
where they belong,

which ones to keep.
and then you have to clear that place
and lift them to it

Then you have to stick to it.
If you don't, if you move it to a temporary refuge

you are lost,
        the alligators will get you and the swamp
        will fill in again.

Nature hates a vacuum.

It will be as if you were in a boat
with no oars, drifting,

waiting for the moon to show up
because you are alone and in the dark
and angry because you

have done it again,
done it to yourself,
as if we were really talking

about clutter and not about time
and not about the drifting emptiness
that we glimpse

that I recognize more each day
that burns my ass and turns me against
myself until I throw that out

the entire thrown together
        accumulated mess of nothing
and nothing and nothing

much at all.
Like me and not the least bit like me
you want to wear alligator shoes

and go dancing until
the sun replaces the moon
and the coolness of the night air

begins to heat.
I will take an order of that.

§

Way Past Midnight

I look at my hands by electric light.
They are becoming the dry wrinkled hands
of an old office man. Not yet my father's hands.
Not my mother's,
which became deflated as she almost made it to 80.
The wrinkles deep,
her skin on her wrists
paper thin,
so fragile when they took the blood tests.
She would bruise like they had used a coal shovel on her.

We should grow old in a big old house
surrounded by grandchildren,
not in the white sheets of the goddamned hospitals
I hate the thought of it.
sitting beside her as her breathing in the coma,
shuddering, slowing
more work for each breath.

I sat in the ugly metal and vinyl padded chair,
my hand under the sheet holding her leg below the knee
her good leg.
Not the left with the stroke twisted ankle,
feeling the warmth of her in my hand
and the shudders of her breathing growing harder
and slower and slowing
to nothing.
Her mouth still open,
the IV pump with saline and the other line morphine.
I listened
and listened for another breath.
Then I walked around to look at her face
half turned from me,
my hand brushing her hair
still brown, just a line or two of grey
then I sat back down in the chair
and put my hand back on her leg below the knee
and felt her warmth and it was quiet, January quiet

Then I got ready to go find a nurse
to check for a pulse, a heartbeat, and to find neither sound,
just the shell still, three days short of her 80th birthday,
and then to tell me that
my mother was dead
officially.

And then the doctor who I had never seen before
came to tell me

that my mother was dead

officially
for the second time.
The doctor a young woman,
younger than me

following her training,
having put on the doctor face
with emotion tucked away,
explained to me that my mother had passed away.
I said, "I know. I was there."

The nurses on the floor looked at me as I waited
for my sister to arrive.
They looked at my face,
my hands spread out, held high,
holding the metal doorframe of the room
so that the building would not explode.
The metal was cool
and had no wrinkles.

DAVID GREEN

DAVID is a lifelong journalist which has included stints as travel writer, book editor and music critic.

He served in the Canadian Army reserves for 34 years, was a creative writing teacher for several years and for 33 years edited and published Green's Magazine.

David is a recent member of The Mariposa Writers' Group, joining in 2010.

Fragments

I liked poetry almost from the start. Grade 2 was it?

On either side the river lie
Long fields of barley and of rye . . .

No, that was Grade 8, *"The Lady of Shallott"*. Mr. McAskill made me memorize the first hundred lines for talking in class. No sooner had I done so than I got nicked with a hundred lines of Browning's *"Herve Riel"*, again for talking in class.

The one in Grade 2, I remember now, began:

Dark brown is the river,
Golden is the sand;
It flows along forever
With trees on either hand.

It was the reading of Wallace Stegner's essay, *"History is a pontoon bridge"* which brought the "long fields of barley and of rye" back in the latest remembrance. Stegner's writing was lucid, provocative, amusing. Besides, he was a Prairie lad.

From a bus window I watched the fields. The brigade-length ranks of potato plants, flanked by rye fields, the potatoes properly at attention, one arm's length between ranks and one between troops, hands stiffly by the seams of the trousers, thumbs forward and fists lightly clenched, toes pointed outward at forty-five degrees, while I, Inspecting General, observed them from the highway and complimented them on their smart appearance and steadiness in the ranks. (At ease, men . . . Three cheers for the general: hip, hip . . .)

Why did *"Dark brown is the river"* stick? Stegner would have recognized that at once. The jungly mud bottom, inadequately flushed by Dauphin Creek, was where my favourite cousins would take me swimming during summer holidays. The creek, with my toes curling in the ooze, came up to my throat.

Once, Cousin Jack caught a little water snake. After that, when I stood in the cool, algaic creek, twiddling toes in the soft mud, I kept a sharp eye for little swimming snakes, and my mouth tightly closed – which was an act of some heroism itself when my nose was stuffy from a cold, as it usually was. To go to the swimming hole alone was a matter of terror; with Jack and the others it was a safer, friendly haven out of the glaring sun and the world of lickings.

Green leaves afloating . . . the poem began its last stanza. Willows, maples and elms snaked and dipped over the creek, and before I could swim I could sail, sail my leaves, my chips of barn shingle or, on good days, a real toy boat.

I got my first jackknife in Grade 1, and it was stolen the first time I brought it to school. "Mrs. Thomas said we must have a teef," I told my best friend at recess. "What's a teef?" But with later blades I became quite good at carving boats. A sucker stick was slotted in as mast (you must be careful not to push it in too far) and a tear of newspaper for the sail.

In the spring runoff I could sail my boats from Pleasant Hill right down to Avenue E – more than a mile. But I had to move quickly and get to the sewer inlets before the boat or it would be sucked down. Sometimes a walk from Pleasant Hill was a three-boat trip.

In the summer we sailed pea-pod canoes stiffened with toothpicks, but they were tippy and not very good in runoff.

Boats of mine aboating, where will all come home? Stevenson, I remember, *A Child's Garden of Verse.*

Mr. McAskill didn't sour me on poetry in spite of *Shallott* and *Herve Riel.* In fact, I grew to like Browning's narrative style so much that I wrote a two-hundred-and-forty-line narrative poem. It did nothing to make me immortal.

Neither did Jeannie McCallum sour me in Grade 6. She gave her strappings with a ruler the first time; I got the leather strap straightaway.

150

I was standing in the cloakroom at the back of the class when Miss McCallum introduced the poem, *The Sea.*
> *The sea, the sea, the open sea;*
> *The blue, the fresh, the ever-free . . .*

I stood in the cloakroom, not because of another punishment for once, but because I'd spilled the ink from my little desk-top well over my trousers. Miss McCallum had sent me back to take off my trousers so that they could dry over the register that also defrosted galoshes. With one hand I anchored myself to a coathook so that I could lean forward, ears projecting beyond the cloakroom wall to hear the teacher, eyes lowered to contemplate the sea-blue stain over my leg. The old tiger bellowed:
> *The sea* (long pause), *the sea;* (dramatic pause)
> *The OPEN* (pause*) sea . . .*

Jeannie McCallum early in the war went away to join the Air Force, and the last I saw of her she was a sergeant, leading a platoon of girls in blue, and bellowing: "Eye-eez RIGHT!" while I suddenly visualized a sea-blue patch of leg.

I liked, too, the poems of calm, of peace. *After School* ended:
> *And there beside an open door,*
> *In a dim country, green and cool,*
> *Her waiting smile shall hear at last:*
> *Mother, I am come home from school.*

This one always made me feel teary. Even in the non-halcyon days of Grade 6 it haunted me. It made me think of Ohio for some reason. When I later visited Ohio for the first time I was disappointed.

But the poem made me think of Mother, too. I associated the last stanza with her telling me to put my toys on the shelf in the closet. (There was an earlier line: *I shall put up my books and games*). Was I memorizing the poem at the time?

I always felt a little sad. Perhaps, for once, I had realized how much of a problem I was to her, and knew on that one day that I had hurt her.

I thought of the lines when I left her for the last time in that last illness, and prayed for the green, cool country to accept her soon, soothing and laving away the hurt.

§

Serenade No. 9 (The Posthorn)

The jaunty birds unheeding sing forever spring,
Though chill the night and leaves crack underfoot;
The flute-cricket chirps against the twilight cling;
The oboe-deer listens, lowers, tastes a root.

The winding-horn unlimbers its clear call:
Violas catch and hearts match its rise.
The hooves unheard thud through our frames withal,
And silv'ry coach flies by to greyhounds' cries.

Yet conjured sight is not the peer of sound,
For your tones speak to deepest soul direct:
Concepts around do not in all redound
And love's wild twisting whim must be suspect.

This paltry paean pen cannot give voice to heart
That echoes sweetest paean of Mozart.

MURIEL HEMMINGS

MURIEL is a mother of four, grandmother of nine and great grandmother of five. Muriel was the daughter of two school teachers who instilled in her the love of reading and writing. As a young wife, she would get no greater pleasure than going camping with the family and wandering off for a few hours to write stories and poetry. Muriel has had some of her work published that include short stories, poetry and craft books. She has often delighted family members by writing a poem to mark a special occasion such as a wedding or birth of a new baby.

For many years, Muriel enjoyed attending the annual Writers' Conference in London. She also received great pleasure from being a member of The Mariposa Writers' Group for many years. More recently Muriel resides at Leisureworld (Spencer House) in Orillia where she continues to author poems for the staff and volunteers. In honour of National Volunteer Week in April, 2011, Muriel wrote a poem that is now proudly displayed in the front foyer of Leisureworld.

A Song for Canada

Canada, land of our heart's adoration
There is no other place where we would live.
Vancouver Island to coast of Newfoundland.
Hope and great freedom you constantly give.

Canada, known for peace-loving reputation
Envied by countries all over the earth.
People are eager to settle in Canada
Even if far from their natural birth.

Canada's first of July's celebration
Remember the day when our nation was born.
Proud to see red maple leaf flag is flying
Silently buried if wind has it torn.

Canada, we are so proud of our Country.
Sharing resources, oil, nickel and gold.
With other countries who purchase our products,
Recognize value wherever they're sold.

Down in the family room sharp darts are hurling.
Which one is known for most accurate aim?
We're free to play hockey, golf, football and curling.
We have lots of fun when we're playing game.

Young folk are free to make plans for their future.
Look forward to life of rewarding careers.
They plan to work hard and to get their promotion,
Relaxing in comfort in their later years.

If you could spend a few days in our country
We feet for certain that you'll understand
Why we're content with the way we are living,
And have no desire to vacate this land.

These are some reasons we show adoration
In Canada country where people are free
To make their own choices, life changing decisions
For making our nation the best it can be.

§

Four Tall Poles

The twelfth of June
The four "sisters" fell
Just why their job is finished
I hardly can tell.

They were trusted as landmarks
On Lake Ontario
Navigators on water
Could tell where to go.

They stood side by side
As a comforting guard.
Those used to their presence
Found losing them hard.

But these are the days
Things are built, and then destroyed.
A patch of land is filled,
Then is quickly left void.

And on West Street South,
They have cleared away turf,
So now we can wonder
What happens with MURF?

§

Guess Who

A row boat cruised on Brewery Bay.
It's owner said, "Here's where I'll stay".

A quiet place where I can ponder
When on these scenic shores I wander.

I could be writing truthful facts
Like business news and Almanacs

But to some folk that might be boring
With no imagination soaring.

Of seriousness I've had my fill
While teaching students at McGill.

I'd rather write stuff that is fun.
Bring happiness to everyone.

I'll call this Mariposa Town.
Activities I'll scribble down

In every person I will mix
A dozen kinds of politics.

My work will stir hatred or fun
Neath Mariposa's shining sun.

I'd like to make all people laugh.
Find fun in every paragraph.

Invent folk like the Reverend Drone
Combining characters I've known.

Cause foks to giggle and not frown
In sunshine sketches of their town.

Bright thoughts like feathers on a peacock.
You've guessed him! He is Stephen Leacock.

§

My Wish for You

I wish you just as many joys
As Sudbury has nickels
As Mr. Heinz has kinds of soup
And Mr. Bick has pickles.

I wish as many thrills as Maxwell
House has beans to roast
And all the pleasures you can spell
In Campbell's alphabet soup

May your friends be as plentiful
As stars up in the sky.
May your romance be luscious
As ice cream and apple pie.

May you be free from pain and problems.
All your aches and hurts be gone
And may your troubles be as rare
As calorie-free desserts!

§

Objects of Pity

I feel so sorry for the crooks
Who trashed a stately home
Who notice shiny Cadillac
And fiercely scratched its chrome.

I sympathize with crazy guys
Who feel a sudden itch
To flex their muscles, shove a car
Into a muddy ditch.

I'm sorry for the goons who start
Those devastating fires.
Who get their kicks in parking lots
By puncturing good tires.

I grieve for fools who war memorials
Harm in dreadful ways
Forgetting that brave soldiers
Had to die in primary days.

I'm sorry for the scoundrels
With no nerve to take the blame
For damaging the monument
Of Samuel de Champlain.

I pity evil enemies
Who feel their task is done
By terrorizing citizens
With deadly bomb or gun.

All mischief makers miss so much
Of earth's short pleasant life.
How can they entertain themselves
By causing all that strife?

Their small minds have a problem
Worse than problems that they cause,
Imagining how smart they are
By disobeying laws.

When caring people, full of love
Find Joy in giving aid
To hungry, homeless persons,
Satisfaction does not fade.

Kind persons who are normal
Try to help folks in distress,
Receive a sense of joy and peace
That gives them happiness.

How thoughtless that these evil folk
Insist they must destroy
Good property. Don't know that they
Deprive themselves of joy.

Volunteers

I have the time to spare
Before bedtime is here
I'll have a friendly chat
With this kindly volunteer

There are telephone friends
I am eager to hear
I can't find their numbers
Please help me volunteer

I slipped on some ice
And the pain was severe
To help me walk safely
I need a volunteer

I'd like to know places
On the TV I hear
I'll borrow a map
From a wise volunteer

I'm bored this dark morning
No sunshine appears
Here's bingo and euchre
With two volunteers

I like to read drama
By William Shakespeare
Can you find me a copy?
I asked a volunteer

Some music we'd like
To bring joy to our ears
We know who can help us
The handsome Paul Spears

It's sad when some seniors
Must shed lonely tears
How comforting when they find
Spiritual volunteers

We residents at Leisureworld
Give loud hearty cheers
Clap hands to show praise
For our great volunteers

CINDY McCARTHY

CINDY was born and raised in the Orillia area and studied journalism at Ryerson Polytechnical in Toronto.

After working for a number of years at community newspapers in the Toronto area, her desire to raise her children closer to her family and live in a more rural setting brought her home. She now lives in Norland, where, whenever time permits, she takes up her pen......

I Fell From the Sky

Once
I was the sun
that warmed their days,
whose beginnings and endings depended solely on my rising and setting.
I was the moon and stars
that filled their sleepy time skies

and I alone could banish their darkness and their things that went
bump in the night.

I was the magic

who made wishes come true and whose kiss healed any hurt.

I could slay their dragons, save the princess, restore the prince, right
the wrongs;

their guard, defender and defeater of evil.
I was their island in the storm and haven from the world;
mender of little hearts and holder of tiny hands.

And I was the happy recipient of all their affections;
butterfly kisses, Eskimo noses,
and hugs that required arms with chubby fists tightly clasped
and legs securely wrapped.
It was to me they brought their wildflower bouquets.
For me hoarded pennies for dollar store bobbles.
It was I to whom they'd run with all their news and every little
thought or emotion.
I was the keeper of secrets and scribe of stories.
For me they'd spend laborious hours with construction paper and scissors
and crayons and glitter glue,
applying buttons and ribbons and macaroni bits and paper hearts;
no effort too great.
The sought after critic. The final word. Teacher. Oracle. Commander in chief.

Now their days rise and fall on other suns.
How then, does one walk the earth, merely mortal,
having once resided at such elevated heights?

Montreal Vignette

I am walking on the street. Mile-End, Montreal. Saturday morning. Sunny. Still early. I feel wonderful.

I'm smiling at the few people I meet. At the shopkeepers. At the passing cars. At nothing in particular.

It's freezing outside and I don't care.

I see her then. She is bundled up from head to foot with only her weathered face – mouth, nose, eyes – showing above her big, woolly, scarf. Toque pulled snug over forehead and ears. She is elderly. She stands motionless. Hands folded in front of her. Staring straight ahead. Why is she here? Standing alone on the street so early in the morning?

As I walk past her I see an empty, paper coffee cup placed carefully at her feet. Now I understand.

I have a hot, foamy, latte in my right hand and six warm, freshly baked croissants in a paper bag in my left. In my pocket, tucked carefully into a tiny, gold, cardboard box is a single heart-shaped chocolate truffle for my son, for which I paid a dollar ten. I'm making my way back to cozy rooms we're occupying during our little weekend excursion to this wonderfully vibrant city. My son waits for me, warmly tuckled into bed. Or maybe by now he has risen and is playing games on his computer to occupy himself until my return.

She has an empty, paper coffee cup.

The street is becoming busy with Hasidic Jews wearing heavy, long, black coats and tall, fur hats, their ringlets dangling at their ears as they hustle their sons off to synagogue. They don't smile back at me. They don't look at her.

I turn back to her then as I search my person for change.

She says, "Bonjour Madame," and meets my glance with the clearest, bluest eyes I've ever seen.

I pour the few coins I have fished out of my pocket into her cup and she says, "Merci. Merci."

She is sincere. She seems grateful. Kind. Straightforward.

I wonder again, "Why is she here. How did she come to be here?"

I tear myself away from her eyes and continue on my way.

I have held one coin back for the parking meter in front of which is parked my almost new truck sitting on four brand new snow tires.

She has an empty paper coffee cup.

What was I thinking? What was I thinking? What *was* I thinking? Why hold one back? I have more coins in my wallet.

I ask myself that age old question (excuse?). "What can I do? I am only one person."

I send up a little prayer for her well being and try to feel better about myself.

§

Visit

I had a visit late last night.
She presented me with one of her famous smiles.
Beautiful and radiant. And welcome.
Like sun, warm on my face through a frigid winter's window pane.
We walked. Down the lane behind their farm.
She is with him now. Loosely clasping the hand of her dearly beloved. Arms swinging.

They walking ahead, me falling behind, I watch them.

High stepping under the shade of aged maples on a sun dappled, two lane, track.

Animated, they chatter and laugh.

Occasionally their voices drift to me on the summer breeze. Whispers, soft as a loved ones warm breath in my ears.

Like a school girl she hop skips. A carefree foot swings at the head of a dandelion gone to seed.

A sudden up-rush of wind blows a hundred softly parachuted teardrops into a cloud.

So when I awoke in the chill quiet before dawn,

I thought not of how still and pale her face was on the pillow in the moments after all her warmth was gone.

I thought of a visit.

Oh, pray, come visit me again.

§

Yellow Butterflies

On her door they placed a yellow butterfly.
No bigger than a splayed matchbook.
Pale. Delicate. Sparkling gaily with glitter.
It bobbed gently on a tiny spring, if the door would swing open or closed.
It proclaimed in silent code to the others not to enter here.

Behind this door lay loss.

Behind this door stood grief. Huddled at the foot of her bed – pale, stunned, and silently screaming pain as if lanced straight through the chest. All in brave face. Grief that wanted to fall to the floor and wail – railing against the loss. Paralyzed. Motion might suggest acceptance of this defeat ... or moving on.

Later they gather at her farm house, sitting cold, in her August kitchen.

Food appears. Delivered by neighbours and friends like silent apparitions. For un-hungry victims, torn from their dreams by a late night call that triggered the pre-dawn scramble to her bedside.

Sorrow hangs heavy and thick in the room. Muffling hushed, voices that make the calls and make the arrangements. In silence, tears burn pallid cheeks.

In the sun-porch a small, yellow butterfly flutters aimlessly about in the sunshine. Softly, soundlessly, bumping screened windows. Cupped hands set it free to the breeze on which it drifts in erratic, clumsy flight.

Later, when another pale, yellow butterfly appears in the sun-porch, it is set free as well. As is the next.

In a few days they will stand together again – gathered at her feet. They will lay her to rest.

The sun will be shining and the day will be perfect. The service – perfect. Everyone there. And strong and brave. As she would have loved.

The wind will rustle the summer grass in which they stand as the priest will say his prayers over her. And no other sounds in this sacred place save the hum of insects and the songs of birds. The scent from flowers, on and around her casket, will fill the air. Among their blossoms flit little, yellow butterflies.

JACQUI MORRISON

JACQUI, author and adult educator, hails from Parry Sound, Ontario.

In 2011, Jacqui Morrison became the Writer in Residence at the Parry Sound Public Library.

In 2008, Lachesis Publishing released her fictional novel, *Kaitlyn Wolfe, Crown Attorney Revised and Edition*. In 2009, she was awarded the Gold IPPY medal for Best Fiction for Central and Eastern Canada for this novel. In 2009, she released a young adult novel called: *Terri's Journey – The Colour of Rain* through Pine & Granite Press. In August 2005, she both contributed to, 'and published' an anthology called *The Sound a Dream Makes* and *Writings from Home and Away.* Jacqui's next mystery/thriller *Oddly Accused* is in the editing process with her publisher, Lachesis Publishing.

Jacqui has facilitated courses in writing for community groups, Canadore College in Parry Sound and groups of youth.

Vignettes of Canada

It rains moderately in Saskatoon. Mervin worries. Will the harvest be enough? Can he and Millie survive?

Nita sits in her log cabin beading a head-dress for the upcoming pow wow —comfortable in solitude. She painstakingly beads, tiny jewel-coloured gems into brushed deer hide, evoking memories from her mother and her mother's mother.

The snow flies rapidly in Nunavut. Harry, the hunter, saddles up with Mary. The winter will be long.

The water of Antigonish is warm and inviting. The Atlantic Ocean is endless. Meanwhile, Mabel throws lobsters into a cauldron of piping hot water. The lobsters shriek as their crust becomes red. Don't worry — Tammy is bringing the pie. Heather has churned her own butter and will arrive soon. Sam will bring his famous lemonade. You're welcome to come.

Sandra swooshes down the mountain through the powdery snow of Whistler, British Columbia in her flashy red ski suit. Her friends follow in playful pursuit. Skiing all day followed by dancing all night. Bliss!

The songs flow from Pierre's accordion as the people congregate in the basement of the white church in St. Laurent, Quebec. His steel-wool hued beard is trimmed, eyes jolly. The square dancing begins as he plays.

The door slides open as Ari comes out to greet his cousin Oreet who is visiting Toronto. The 9-hour flight from Israel has tired the elderly man. They embrace and enjoy afternoon tea.

It's people greeting people, needing people that define our Canada, our home.

Stained Glass/Shattered Glass

At first glance
the encounter
was like the forming of
a stained-glass window

She the jeweller
who etched the picture
envisioned the unique
image

He the craftsman
devoted to being the best
poured molten lead
formed the frame

She – a dreamer
an intellectual
born into a situation
so melancholy but so exceptional

She worked on her glass
tenaciously
whilst he became angry.
What held them together?

Was she disloyal?
Dreaming of another life
being alone
yearning for — Serenity

One day, she woke up
stared at the stained-glass window
six feet wide
and three feet high

It sparkled
A Kaleidoscope of rainbow hues
Glistened in the sun
Remarkable in the rain

People came from everywhere
to see the stained-glass window
inspiring Awe
innate beauty

But five years ago
spider cracks formed
hardly noticeable
diminutive

One day
not very long ago
the glass shattered
Imploded

She felt the sensation
from afar
shards of glass
Icicles on the lawn

Cut into her heart
from a distance
an ocean apart
Yet in the same home

She stood
hands covered
in the sparkling glass
Radiant in it

Immune to the pain
free of the grief
Ready
to begin

A new glass
perhaps a small one
with no one to pour the lead

She didn't need — Him
She needed
her own healing
Heart

ANNE O'ROURKE

ANNE was born in 1935 in Germany. She wrote her memoir about growing up in "interesting times" in Berlin. She wanted to pass this on to her children and grandchildren. Her training, as a Dress Designer in Germany, provided her with the necessary qualifications to teach Pattern Drafting at Seneca College in Toronto.

Anne is now retired and living in Moonstone where she writes poetry of day-to-day events in her life. She volunteers to help persons with disabilities and heart and stroke survivors in Orillia. Anne also plays the accordion for the Black Forest Singers in Barrie. She hikes, bikes and canoes with the Ganaraska Hiking Club.

And I Never Saw Her Face

Who is that stranger, in the bed next to mine?
the curtain around her drawn tight.
I cannot see her, but I know she is there,
she was moaning and crying all night.
Who is that stranger, and how can I help?
she is suffering so close to me.
What is her story? And why is she here?
and what is her history?
Now the first daughter came
and brought two little girls,
who still believe grandma gets better.
They kiss and they hug her,
but cannot stay quiet,
they are young and they chitter and chatter.
Daughter 2 comes later
and she begged for forgiveness,
and it hurts me to hear her cry.
She has many regrets,
and she finds it now hard,
to say her final goodbye.
Then the third daughter came,
and she brought the pastor.
They talked quietly, and started to sing.
The nurses all came, they stood still and just listened,
to the most beautiful church hymn.
What happened to her I will never know
a new patient took her place.
They took her away while I was asleep,
----and I NEVER SAW HER FACE.

Life Is a Journey

Life is a journey---it is like a train,
With new vistas after each bend.
Life is a journey---you must fully observe it,
You have choices, it's all in your hand.
With correct precision, the train can go slow,
You feel safe, but after a while,
You get bored, and you start to question,
Is this all, is this now my style?
Life is an adventure, and you have to decide,
'Cause the train stays straight on its track.
It has so many stops, and it is up to you,
To stay with it, or rather turn back.
Life is a challenge, live each day to its fullest,
And don't be afraid to choose wrong.
Try everything, experience all,
It builds character, you end up strong.

§

Mother Earth

Mother Earth cried out, "You are hurting me,"
The greed of mankind has to end.
You went too far, you wanted too much,
Stop it now---or I never will mend.
I gave you fresh water, to water your crops,
And all kinds of fish to eat.
But this was not enough, and you wanted much more,
There's never an end to your greed.
You polluted the water, and cut down the trees,
This in turn eroded the soil.
You dug deep in my inside, to take out the coal,

You drilled holes to remove the oil.
So I started to rumble, to give you some warning,
This changed nothing, you did not stop.
So I had to explode, and I killed many people,
Spewing fire out of my top.
I pushed underground plates, which created an earthquake,
A Tsunami swept whole towns away.
So many were killed, and all the survivors
Had no food, and no place to stay.
You don't need the threat of a Nuclear Reactor,
To create electricity.
You have free wind for windmills,
And plenty of sun, for solar energy.
So let's work together, cut down our lifestyle,
And hope that we have success.
Future generations will be thankful
If we now clean up the mess.

§

Smorgasbord

TIP-TAP----TIP-TAP----TIP-TAP-----TIP
I think I heard a mouse.
TIP-TAP----TIP-TAP----TIP-TAP----TIP,
It's somewhere in the house.
I hope it's not a family,
I hope it's only one,
Because the way, the mice do breed,
We could be overrun.
They did come in, when it turned cold
They like it nice and warm,
And all the snow, we have right now,
Would only do them harm.
But when it's quiet, and I can't sleep,

And hear the TIP and TAP.
I finally decided and went out and bought a trap.
Next morning I had the result,
One mouse was now all dead.
Was lying on the wooden board,
After the cheese it had.
To rid us of this ugly sight,
I picked all up and threw it out
Into the winter night, into the ice and snow.
And who was thankful later on?
It was a hungry cat,
Out on the prowl to look for food
Happy now to be fed.
And you have to admit, on a cold winter night
There is nothing better to eat,
Off a wooden board, out in the snow,
Than a chunk of freshly killed meat.

EVELYN N. POLLOCK

EVELYN's childhood dream was to become a teacher. She fulfilled this dream and much more. Along the way, she kept a journal, jotting down unique and quirky experiences, always planning to write a book or two in later years.

Her early career included teaching for the City of Toronto and then serving as an elected Trustee, Vice-Chair and Chair of the City of York Board of Education, where she was an advocate for gender and racial equality.

Life after politics included twenty-five years as a Human Rights Consultant. For fifteen of those years she was President of her own management consulting firm, Pollock Consulting Ltd. Over the years Evelyn wrote many training manuals and business articles.

In 2009, Evelyn retired early to pursue her life-long interests of painting and writing. Since retiring, she has written many short stories and has a couple of books 'in the works'.

Evelyn is the current President of the Orillia Fine Arts Association, an active member of the Mariposa Writers' Group, a member of the Writers' Cauldron, and a four-time veteran of the Muskoka Novel Marathon. *"Life is good and genetics indicate that I may have many more years of creative living ahead. I thank David, my wonderful husband and best friend, for encouraging me to follow my dreams .... And, I thank my terrific children for providing me with lots of great material for my short stories!!"*

AND ALL WILL BE WELL -

If Valerie hadn't received the call from her daughter, she would have kept her promise to herself and driven straight home. She knew the sale was still on at Pier 1 Imports. On her last visit she had acquired a room full of new wicker furniture for her solarium and the thought that she might have missed some treasure on her last visit ate at Valerie's gut. But, in truth, the last thing she needed was more stuff.

It wasn't just Valerie's condo that was full to bursting. Her trusty van was stuffed with the flotsam and jetsam of her life. A man's black cashmere overcoat, freshly dry-cleaned, hung from a hook over the rear passenger door. Her 92-year-old aunt, Jessie, had passed it on, suggesting that maybe Valerie's son, Kevin, could use the coat to keep him warm while he panhandled on the streets of Toronto. Sure, a panhandler in a cashmere coat – that would go over well.

Aunt Jessie had also given Valerie a yellowed copy of Dr. Spock's *Baby and Child Care* for her daughter Rachel. This was more of a hint rather than for any immediate need, as Rachel was neither pregnant, nor planning to get pregnant, nor engaged, although she and her current boyfriend had been living together for two years.

Heaped in the back seat of Valerie's van were unopened Home Depot boxes containing sets of kitchen and bathroom faucets, a microwave, a cappuccino machine, as well as strips of quarter round and six brass coat hooks all destined for her new condo.

Discretely tucked under the front passenger seat was a pillowcase full of old prayer shawls and prayer books that Valerie's 95-year-old father had 'borrowed' from various synagogues. Valerie hadn't yet figured out how to give them back without humiliating her dad.

In the trunk were Valerie's Canadian Tire purchases from the previous day: twenty-four plastic clothes hangers; eight knives set in a wooden block; and six rolls of Christmas wrapping paper covered with smiling Santas, something every Jewish family should have on hand. Valerie planned to move all of this into her new condo that day.

She was just a block shy of Pier 1 Imports when her cell phone rang.

"Mom!" her daughter Rachel announced through the Bluetooth speaker. "He said he *never* wants to get married. *Ever.*"

Rachel vented. Valerie made soothing noises.

What is wrong with men today? Valerie thought.

Well, Valerie had no choice but to pull into the Pier 1 parking lot. This wasn't a call she could handle while driving.

Rachel's last two serious boyfriends had gone right to the edge with her – proposed, bought her engagement rings. But boyfriend number one thankfully had come out of the closet the day after he'd gotten down on his knees. Boyfriend number two had waited till after Valerie had paid the non-refundable deposit for the reception hall. Then he'd phoned Rachel to say he was backing out to travel the world. It could have been worse, Valerie supposed. He could have texted Rachel from Thailand.

Sexy, brilliant and successful, her Rachel had no trouble attracting men. But apparently, when it came to marriage, Rachel was cursed.

After Rachel's call, Valerie felt punch drunk as she stumbled from her van and promptly stepped into the first slush of the season. Swearing at herself for not wearing boots and cursing her daughter's current boyfriend for being a self-centred thirty-year-old adolescent, Valerie thought, *If only I could put the evil eye on him and make him move out, so that Rachel can move on.*

And that's when something shiny caught Valerie's eye. Not sure what it was, she bent down and scooped it up between her thumb and forefinger.

It was a ring. It was dirt-encrusted, flattened and with no shine to the centre stone or to the four chips set in silver filigree around it. They could have been bits of yellowed glass or, for all she knew about gems, they might have been perfect diamonds. The style was old-fashioned, the filigree elaborate. Possibly a fake she decided. Or maybe not?

Valerie scanned the parking lot to see if anyone was searching for a lost item. No luck. She grabbed a pen and paper from her purse and scribbled a quick note, '*If you lost a ring, contact me.*' She added her name and phone number before slipping the message under the wiper of the windshield of the SUV parked next to her. Surprisingly, there were no other cars at that end of the lot. Then she slowly walked away and through the front entrance of Pier I Imports. As she entered, she tucked her find into her jacket pocket.

Guilt was one of the gifts of her upbringing. Valerie immediately approached a cashier and asked if anyone had reported a lost ring. Several clerks gathered around but none of them recalled a report of a lost ring.

An overly zealous sales clerk labeled *Jimmy* called out, "What does it look like lady? Can I see it?"

Valerie thought but didn't say, *Do you think I'm an idiot! Sure I'll show it to you, you slimy jerk, and then you'll have your girlfriend call me tomorrow to claim it.*

Valerie left the ring in her pocket. She was the cautious sort and hadn't fully processed the significance of her find.

"It looks like a lady's wedding ring," she told the curious clerks. "But it's just as likely to be costume jewellery. It could have fallen out of a crackerjack box, for all I know."

Valerie asked the cashier to place a note in the store window, but was told it was against store policy. So, Valerie wrote down her name and phone number and the cashier agreed to post it in the back, where all employees could see it.

Out of habit, Valerie quickly circumnavigated the store. Although her eyes were busy scanning the shelves for bargains, her thoughts were on the ring in her pocket and on what her find might mean.

'*Bashert*' is the Yiddish word for destiny, it was '*meant to be*'. That is how Valerie interpreted this event – she was meant to find this ring. It was a sign. Perhaps her daughter Rachel would finally get a permanent engagement ring. Had she not just been talking to Rachel about her problems with men? Perhaps it was a sign that Valerie's son Kevin would improve and find and marry the girl of his dreams - someone like his ex-girlfriend Brittany.

But Valerie couldn't bear to consider that. Kevin's problems were so deep, so complex, that they defied comprehension, much less solution. At least once a week Valerie and her husband would visit Kevin on his favourite street corner. They found him a place – his own small apartment. He didn't stay. They continued to bring him clean clothes, but he went about in rags. Always, on Fridays, they brought Kevin food – his favourites from when he was a boy. "Thanks, Mom," he'd say. Sometimes he'd eat what they brought. Usually not - he'd trade it for cigarettes or drugs.

Valerie took Kevin to the hospital for treatment but they just let him go. Perhaps they were right. He usually had the sense to get in out of the cold and he wasn't injuring himself or others out there on his favourite corner. He wasn't happy of course. But neither was he terribly sad. It's more like he was only half alive - a lost soul, a stranger begging on the corner of Spadina and College.

When Valerie finally got home, she rummaged through her dresser to find the miniature silver jewelry box she'd bought in Venice years before and placed the ring inside. Then she placed the silver box inside the zippered compartment of her oversized purse. There the ring would be safe until she found the owner. Surely the owner was looking for it. A ring like that was a significant piece of jewellery: an engagement ring from her parent's era, or a special anniversary gift – a piece of jewellery valued beyond price … if it was real.

Thoughts of that ring never left Valerie's mind. She scoured the newspapers and periodically went online to search for notices of lost jewellery.

Days passed, weeks passed and then months passed. The ring remained unclaimed and hidden inside the silver box, inside her handbag.

Finally, Valerie took the ring to a jeweller she trusted. The claws were tightened, the ring was cleaned, and the band was straightened. The jeweller confirmed that it was a substantial diamond set in platinum. Valerie didn't have the courage to ask for an appraisal. In any case, she didn't need one. Now she knew for a certainty that the ring was real.

If only I could find the owner, she thought.

Though it sparkled invitingly, Valerie couldn't bring herself to wear the ring. Nor could she imagine selling it. Once again the ring went into the silver box and into her purse.

Meanwhile, life continued much the same as before. Kevin continued to beg at his street corner. Rachel continued to waste another year of her life with the boyfriend who would never marry her. And Valerie had almost given up on finding the ring's owner.

Then, out of the blue, Valerie got a phone call from Kevin's former girlfriend. Brittany wanted to know if Kevin was okay.

Valerie had loved Brittany for the happiness that she had brought to Kevin's life. For a time, Brittany had provided stability and direction for Kevin, giving him unconditional love. Brittany was Kevin's constant support, thinking for him, planning for him and carrying him through that phase of his life, as Valerie had always done in his earlier years.

On the surface, everything looked good and for once, after so many years of turmoil, Valerie and her husband came to believe that Kevin had started to turn his life around… until he paid the deposit on an engagement ring and Brittany accepted his proposal. They chose a large showy platinum ring with a centre Zircon and real diamond baguettes, planning to replace the centre stone with a real diamond in the future.

Brittany and Rachel, who was also engaged at the time, began buying wedding magazines and talking endlessly about bridal gowns and wedding locations. For a few months life was wonderful. It seemed that Valerie's family would expand and flourish.

But things had fallen apart. Rachel's fiancé backed out to travel the world. As for Kevin and Brittany, Valerie was not certain what really happened between them.

Much later, when the threatening letters started arriving from a collection agency, Valerie learned that the platinum ring had cost Kevin $4,500, even without a real centre diamond. Kevin had put down $1,000 and monthly payments were to follow; except Kevin had never made another payment. After their break-up a few months later, both Kevin and the ring disappeared.

At the end of the telephone call, Valerie thanked Brittany for phoning and thanked her for loving Kevin. Then she pulled the little silver jewellery box out of her purse for another look.

Rings can have so many stories. Was the owner of this one young, old, engaged, married, or widowed? Was the ring stolen? The more Valerie considered the provenance of that ring the more inventive she became.

That New Year's Eve, Valerie and her husband hosted a dinner party for friends. Two criminal lawyers, an environmental lawyer, a real estate lawyer, a doctor, and an artist sat around the dining table.

While they ate their dessert, Valerie posed a hypothetical question, "What would you do if you were walking along the street, looked down and found a Rolex watch?"

The question was a hit. Her guests bantered back and forth about how much effort they would put into finding the real owner and when exactly the Rolex would become theirs. The environmental lawyer argued you wouldn't have to do a thing. The owner would have to find his own bloody watch and if he didn't find it in a reasonable time – the watch was yours. The criminal lawyers agreed, pointing out that the person who lost the watch had likely claimed the insurance money.

"Finders keepers?" Valerie asked.

"You bet. It's the law," they all replied.

Then Valerie told them the true story and everything she had done over the past couple of years to find the ring's owner.

"It's yours," they all assured her. Free and clear."

Valerie nodded, but didn't agree. You see, she is still waiting on fate, believing that one afternoon she will be sitting at a table at some event and a charming elderly woman, recently widowed, will turn to her and tell her a story about that horrible day when she lost her beautiful filigreed engagement ring that her late husband had given her over 60 years before.

Then Valerie will pull the little silver jewellery box from her purse and remove the lid to reveal the ring. And all will be well. It is *Bashert*...

Chance Meeting

It was a Thursday morning in July and there was a severe heat alert as Samantha backed her new car out of the garage. Both the air-conditioner and the car radio were on full blast as she headed to town for her weekly Weight Watchers' meeting. She hadn't lost much since joining six weeks earlier. Her excuses included too many neighbourhood get-togethers, a wedding, and a retirement party. The truth was that it was just damned hard saying no to a craving.

Twenty minutes later, Samantha pulled her car into a parking spot outside the meeting venue. She lightened up, removing her watch, dangling earrings, and bracelet, carefully placing them into the cup holder next to her refillable Tim Horton's mug.

Samantha locked her car and dashed inside to line up behind women and men of all sizes, anxiously awaiting their moment of truth. Her turn came soon enough. Not so pleased with herself, but happy to have avoided complete humiliation, Samantha stepped off the scale, registering a resounding new weight loss of four ounces. She imagined a volume of fat equivalent to four slices of processed cheese eliminated from her body.

When the meeting ended, Samantha stepped outside into the parking lot and considered going out for a bite to eat. *What is the POINTS value of a Greek salad? If I have the salad, can I resist a slice of cheesecake for dessert?*

Just as her resolve began to weaken, she noticed a young man approaching. Her first thought was that he was there to pick up his mother after the meeting. Then she noticed him trying to catch her eye.

"Hi." He gave her an attractive, full-toothed, cigarette-stained smile and opened his left hand to show a ten dollar bill and some loose change.

A familiar pain shot through Samantha's heart.

"I'm trying to get enough money together to buy a bus

ticket back home to Sudbury. Could you help me?" he continued.

Samantha knew that the town bus station was twenty minutes away by car. She also knew that face – young, well-mannered, smart in a worldly way, cheeks slightly sunken, skin pale. He wore an open shirt over a not too clean t-shirt and his cargo shorts were slightly tattered. He could have been a high school or college student on summer break.

"Don't think so – you're pretty far from the bus station," Samantha answered, to buy some thinking time.

He stretched himself up to his full height of maybe five foot ten and his tone hardened. "It's the truth. I come from Sudbury and I just want to go home to my family."

God, he's young, Samantha thought. Her hand fumbled in her open purse for some change as she tried to figure out her strategy.

"Please don't lie to me," she begged as she looked into his eyes. "Your cheeks are sunken. I know that look. I've seen it before. What are you using – oxycontin, crack, heroin? I'll give you some money, but only if you tell me the truth."

He hesitated for a few seconds, holding Samantha's gaze. Then he looked away and answered, "Cocaine powder."

"You mean crack cocaine?"

He seemed surprised as he nodded in response.

"That's pretty addictive – really hard to stop. Have you ever tried to stop?" she asked in a gentle voice.

"I tried to get into Detox a couple of times, but they were full. Sometimes I want to stop. But once I use, I just want it again." He reached into his shirt pocket and pulled out a half-smoked cigarette and a lighter. She noticed his yellow stained fingers.

Samantha had another flashback – an open drawer filled with cigarette stubs, cigarette papers, tobacco remnants, all collected from the pavement. Her stomach rolled.

187

"I know that story – you're an addict. You're on welfare, aren't you?"

He nodded.

"You get your welfare cheque and head to Money Mart to cash it, right? Spend it all on drugs in the first weekend and then you don't have any money left for rent or for food for the rest of the month?" She was direct, not accusatory, speaking to him as if she knew him well.

Samantha watched the confident shine go out of his eyes as he nodded again.

A flashback took Samantha to the side door of a down-town church. She could see the piles of dirty clothing, the empty Tim Horton cups, the rotting fast food containers, and the damp, empty sleeping bag resting on the snow on that freezing night. That memory was etched forever in her mind, but now she couldn't find her brother Greg in the picture.

"Hey, lady, are you going to help me out or not?" his bravado was back.

"Where do you live? Are you homeless?" she asked, remembering Greg.

"Nah - I crash with my ex-girlfriend. She's pretty fed up with me, but I'm okay for now. I still have a place to stay."

Samantha's protective instinct was on the loose. "Can you call your parents in Sudbury and ask for their help. Would they help you?"

He hesitated for a second. "Maybe they would help. My mom used cocaine too, but my dad doesn't. My grandma used to let me stay with her, but she's dead now. She left me $5,000.00 and my parents shipped her walnut dresser down here. She wanted me to have it. I spent the money, but the dresser is at my ex's apartment. Maybe you need a dresser? It's real nice."

"I'm sorry your grandmother died", answered Samantha.

"I'm sure you meant a lot to her if she left you money and her dresser. You should keep it."

"Yeah – maybe", his eyes were already scanning the empty parking lot for another mark.

"I think I have some information in my car that might help you", she said, trying to keep his attention.

For years, Samantha had carried a list of rehabilitation centre phone numbers in her glove compartment, just in case. But she knew she hadn't transferred the list into her new car. She went through the motions of unlocking her car door and fumbling through her papers anyway, to keep him there just a little longer.

"I really have lived your story," she said. "My brother Greg fooled around with drugs. He was three years older than me. He was brilliant – everybody's favourite. In our day it was hashish, magic mushrooms and LSD. I do know your story. I've been there. How old are you?"

He looked so young and innocent. She remembered that look.

"Twenty-one… I've only been doing this for a couple of years. I'm not really an addict."

"My name's Samantha, but you can call me Sam. What's your name?" she asked, not really expecting the truth.

"Chance."

"Chance, you can have a better life without drugs, if you decide that's what you really want." She couldn't stop herself from preaching. She still hadn't handed him any money and his eyes and body were beginning to move restlessly. It was 12:55 p.m. They had been talking for less than ten minutes.

"Where's your brother now? Is he still doing drugs?" Chance asked, but she could tell he was only feigning interest.

"Greg and I used to pretend we could fly when we were little kids. We would jump from the sofa to a chair in the living room and imagine the wind carrying us up and back down. I got over it, but Greg always dreamed that he could fly. Greg started to experiment with drugs the summer he finished high school – he had a full scholarship for university, but he never finished. He loved his drugs – in the end he was on the street. He was twenty-four when he jumped off a bridge onto the highway. Some said it was suicide – I knew he was just trying to fly."

Chance's eyes widened.

"Look, I'll be back here next week at the same time. I'll bring phone numbers of local rehab centres with me. I'll wait right here for you between 12:45 and 1:00 p.m. If you come, you come…"

"I'll be here at one o'clock next Thursday," Chance answered. For a nanosecond, he probably meant it.

Samantha dropped a five dollar bill into his hand. "Hope to see you next week," she said, then climbed into her car and started the engine.

As she made her turn out of the lot onto the side street, Samantha spotted him heading for a telephone booth.

Calling his drug dealer, she thought. But she prayed he was calling his parents.

The eternal optimist, Samantha, spent the following Wednesday evening searching the internet and updating her list of addresses and phone numbers of drug rehabilitation programmes in the area. She stuffed the list into a large, envelope and wrote *For Meeting with Chance* on the outside.

The next morning, following her Weight Watchers' meeting, Samantha stood out in the parking lot waiting for him with the envelope in her hand. The time came and went.

Of course he was nowhere to be seen. At 1:30 p.m., Samantha folded the envelope and placed it back in the glove compartment of her car. If there was ever a next time, she would be prepared.

Part Two

Months later, on the west side of town, a block from the lakeshore, tucked safely into his tiny, rented basement room, Chance crouched shivering on his bare mattress. His bruised arms were clutched tightly around his aching knees. His once sky-blue eyes, now murky and bloodshot, stared at the walls, unseeing. Heart pounding irregularly in his chest, he rocked from side-to-side to vanquish the waves of searing pains in his joints. Puddles of sweat drenched his already stained t-shirt.

Out of place in the tomb-like room, the polished antique walnut dresser called softly to him in his grandmother's honeysuckle voice, warming him, surrounding him in her fleshy, loving arms. The walnut dresser was solid. It was hers. It was the only remaining physical evidence of his real life – the life before this room.

A sudden, cool breeze blew through the small, unscreened window, rattling the metal blinds and startling him into the present. His vision cleared for a fraction of a second, long enough for his eyes to settle on the government-issued, beige envelope lying open beside him on the bed – just long enough for him to grasp how the contents could instantly take his terrible pain away.

Desperately, he stretched his legs, pulled his month-end welfare cheque from the envelope, shoved his bare feet into his damp, worn running shoes and rose to his full height of 5'10", his head grazing the base of the broken ceiling fan. He took three steps to the door of his minuscule room, pulled it open and moved his emaciated body down the narrow hallway, past the shared, makeshift bathroom with the exposed pipes and rusting tub, past the kitchenette with the missing stove and dripping faucet, up the stairs, out the side door of the building and onto the street.

The walnut dresser stood by helplessly, watching, while the essence of his grandmother flowed after him, aching to hold him and love him back to health.

Chance lumbered mindlessly down the long block of apartments, not hearing the sounds of babies crying, mothers soothing their children, or dogs barking. Propelled by the only reward that meant anything to him, he focused on his mission, at first not noticing the police cruiser that slowed down behind him and then followed along at the speed of his strides.

Once aware of the shadow beside him, Chance focused his eyes down on his filthy running shoes, ignoring the double set of judging eyes in the cruiser beside him. He hummed silently under his breath, still shivering and fighting the pains as he slowed his pace, trudging on, repeating his silent mantra: *Hold steady. Don't look at them. You didn't do anything wrong. They have no right to stop you. You are a free man. You have a right to be here.*

As he turned the corner onto Lakeshore Avenue, the cruiser pulled away, but the judging eyes still burned through him, taunting him. For once they didn't stop him, as they had so many times before just because they could.

Someone watching would say that poverty draws attention, makes you obvious, and makes you guilty just by your presence in the world. Chance knew this from experience, but at that moment, he was a wealthy man. He still had his grandmother's walnut dresser and he had his cheque.

Just ahead, the familiar Money Mart sign shone brightly, enticing him. At that moment, nothing else was visible to Chance. His rent became a distant memory with each step he took closer to that door. Memories of the street and homelessness did not haunt him, only the promise of the absence of pain called him forward.

For only a second, a dim memory of a brief encounter with a woman named Samantha flashed across his mind.

Rule of Thumb

The rising column of steam from the whistling kettle settled in tiny droplets on the cabinet above the kitchen counter. Marion watched vacantly, as her right index finger drew the initials KMA across the damp cabinet door.

Startled by the sudden shrill ring, Marion moved quickly across the vinyl kitchen floor to grab her cell phone from the counter. She snapped the phone open anticipating silence on the other end. The words *unknown number* appeared on the screen. Marion pushed the missed call button – forty-three calls from an unknown caller since midnight. Her stomach was in knots. Her heart pounded against her ribcage. Bile rose in her throat.

Marion backed away from the counter with rigid determination. She knew this would never stop until she submitted to his control. Even then she knew he would continue to suffocate her with his demands and suspicions.

Marion unplugged the boiling kettle, placed a tea bag in her ceramic mug and poured in the boiling water, counting to twenty, until the water turned a brilliant amber colour. As she turned, she caught a glimpse of her bruised reflection in the mirror above the kitchen table.

Resolutely she reached down into the pocket of her apron and pulled out a small plastic vial, unscrewed the lid and emptied the powdery substance into her tea and stirred vigorously.

A smile spread across Marion's face. An inner peace calmed her as she pulled out the kitchen chair and settled into it. She continued to sip her tea and trace the initials KMA on the table top as the soothing warmth slowly spread through her body.

"Kiss My Ass" she laughed, as she faded from consciousness.

Michael pushed the *redial* button on his office desk. His

remorse was receding as his anger rose. He stared down at his large hands as he repeated the definition from his British law book, "***Rule of Thumb****: the measure of the stick that you can use to beat your wife*".

In his mind, he had acted within the law. Eventually, Marion would come to understand. Michael would make sure of that.

MARILYN (CORNELIUS) RUMBALL

MARILYN was born and raised in Kingston, Ontario, attended school there and graduated from Queen's University with a degree in Psychology, Political & Economic Sciences. During her years at Queen's, she was a feature writer for the *Queen's Journal* and *Lavana Editor*. Following graduation, Marilyn was employed by Atomic Energy of Canada as assistant to the Medical Director, doing research in the medical uses of radioactive isotopes, speech writing and preparing précis of various medical articles for future research.

Marilyn came to Orillia with her husband when he accepted a position with Fahralloy Canada Ltd. At the same time, Pete McGarvey hired Marilyn to write continuity (commercials) for Radio Station CFOR. She eventually learned to do a little of everything, including camera work and proofreading for Smith Printing, which was a branch of CFOR for a short time.

When CFOR was sold, Marilyn returned to University for her teaching certificate and began a long career at Park Street Collegiate teaching English, Business Subjects and even Grade 13 Family Studies for several years. She eventually became the Director of the Business Department.

Meanwhile, back on the farm, Marilyn was involved in breeding Canadian Hunters, taking her children to Horse Shows and becoming a Senior Recognized Judge with Equine Canada. She is a life member of the Canadian Sport Horse Association and her life-long interest in horses continues.

Despite a very busy life, Marilyn still finds time to write, but now it is mostly poetry and short stories. She is an active member of the Stephen Leacock Association and Chair of the Student Humorous Short Story Competition. Marilyn is also a founding member of the Mariposa Writers' Group.

Last Day at Devon

The yellow gate swings slowly,
Dust stirs and eddies,
Paper drifts, soars and drops,
Flattened against the fence.
The deserted show grounds rest
As the last riders leave for home.
Across the empty yard laughter rings clear,
A horse neighs and stamps,
A washroom door slams; a tailgate is lifted
Truck doors close, and the laughter is gone.
I am alone.
Alone to enjoy this bittersweet moment
That is the end of every show.
I sit listening to the silence
Sharing this time of sweet sadness with
The ghosts of unrealized dreams
Then, wrapped in an evening breeze

Redolent of fresh hay, I walk through the yellow gate into the summer night
and I too, am gone.

New Beginnings

Can you feel it?
The first breeze of evening
Wandering softly,
Cool fingers
Tracing lines of love
On warm skin
Touching our souls.
It awakens the flower
Growing slowly within me
Though still we lie
Unclothed, unmoving,
Unwilling to let the present
Become the past
Yet craving an ending,
For the flower to unfold
And fill the night.

The Rats in My Classroom Were Not Always the Kids

Teaching is the best! Every day is different. It's like being the star in a play you have never read – you have no idea of the plot or your lines. Well, you think you do when the class begins; you've planned your lesson. But your students have their own agendas.

Early in my teaching career I decided I would not allow myself to be "thrown" by anything that happened. Snakes in drawer? I didn't know how, but I would deal with it. I really hadn't thought of rats. But it was rats that appeared in my accounting class.

In the middle of my dissertation on some very important aspect of 'debit equals credit', I saw the rat! It crawled across a desk and hopped down onto the floor. With great aplomb, I marched down the aisle, lifted the hairy beast under his arms and held him up.

"Whose rat is this?" I asked.

Immediately, one of the girls screeched and climbed up on her chair. She didn't actually say "EEK" but it was a close relative. I was shaking inside myself; I had never touched a rat and had never planned to.

"I'm allergic," said the young man who had recently shaved his head. He pulled his shirt up to cover his baldness.

"Watch out", said the leather-clad young lady – the one the boys called 'the biker's girl' – "that rat is going to urinate all over you!"

"How do you know?" I asked in my "stupid" voice.

"I have a cage full at home. They're hooded rats; they're awesome pets! Look there, see, his bladder is full."

"Wow!" the class clown yelled, "Is that fellow ever hung!"

"Give him to me," said 'Biker Girl', "I'll take him next door and hang him over the Bradley!"

With a swish of leather and a clanking of chains, the girl and the rat left the room. I couldn't think of any way to associate this activity with my lesson on interest payments on used cars, so I did the best I could.

"Whose rat was that?" I asked again.

I looked toward the desk where the rat had first appeared. I looked at the girl who occupied that desk, the girl who had become known to the class as 'el freako' since the day she attacked 'class clown', stabbing him in the neck with her ball point. Out from under her long, curly hair crawled a second rat.

"Janice," I asked, "did you drive your boyfriend's truck here today?"

"Yes."

"Then, when Anika comes back, you take your rats and drive them right back home! "And Fern," I said, sternly, "Get down off that chair!"

Anika thumped into the room in her Doc Martin's and handed the rat back to me.

"He feels much better now," she said.

Janice collected her rats and flounced out the door. The bell rang, and Act One was over.

We were having mini commencement that afternoon. I was due to appear on stage, but decided to drop by the Principal's office on my way to the auditorium.

"I sent Janice home," I told him. "With her rats!" His mouth dropped. "I thought that would be better than sending her here to the office. I'm not sure she left with them, so if you look out over the crowd and see rats running down the aisle, well, we better have some plan in mind."

Janice did appear for commencement, but if she had her rats with her, she kept them well concealed in her hair. Act Two was a great disappointment. We had our lines ready but didn't get to use them! The Play is never the one you rehearsed.

CHRISTINE SPEAR

CHRISTINE says that all her life she has been surrounded by people who love the English language. Given that she's easing into the retirement zone, that's a lot of people. They were her family, her Ex, English, Drama and Transformational teachers and, of course, her two writing groups: The Mariposa Writers' Group and The Writer's Cauldron. These people supported her by reading, singing and writing around her. They were and are encouraging, candid and wise, always with a view to improving her writing. A long nursing career, a long path to her son in Peru and a long list of funny happenings coupled with a bizarre imagination provide the fodder for her stories. As yet she hasn't limited herself to one genre or form; even the odd poem slips out.

Christine's main writing goal is to entertain with stories but she also likes to explore writing social commentary. She writes for the voice and pieces to be read out loud. One of her greatest joys is to be asked to read one of her pieces.

Lion: A Fantasy (Maybe)

It was a November 'soup-for-lunch' day when I set off for Coopers Falls Road and the woods of Crown Land near it. Only once, had I ever been this way. Badgering my friend daily as to the exact spot of the cougar sighting gleaned me nothing.

I'm Janet Grove, Nurse, with an inclination to the bizarre. This trip convinced me of that.

No one could be talked into going with me. They preferred watching nature at home on High Definition while snuggled in a quilt. The drizzle postponed all their outings 'til May.

I was fiercely drawn to this cat even though my friend had said she'd never been so scared in her life. This baffled me as she had two dogs, two friends and two tons of car between her and it.

Leaves still clung to the trees but they were losing the battle. Still, the wilderness deepened. I pulled into an abandoned lane – now on Crown Land.

Laughing, I was reminded of heroines who set off to an attic to investigate strange sounds. Never once are they armed with AK- 47s and neither was I.

Sitting in my car, I scanned the woods. It was a silly notion to think that a mountain lion was still around. The paw prints the Ministry of Natural Resources required for I.D were not inside my car so I got out.

Standing there smelling the freshness, I slowly became aware I wasn't alone. My heart rate tripled. How I wanted back in the car! Curiously, I stood like a statue.

My eyes scanned the woods again. They fixed on a huge cat staring back at me. Then without a sound we talked.

He said, "I knew you'd come. Yes, I'm a mountain lion, Felis concolor as science would have it--cougar, puma, painter and more. Though these days, you're more apt to be called a cougar. And no! We won't eat you."

"We", I stammered, then spotting a tawny she-lion emerging from the bush.

With courage I did not feel I said, "How did you know I'd come?"

"You don't know yourself very well do you?" He quipped.

Pretending I knew myself very well, thank you, I changed the subject scolding,

"How could you be so stupid as to let yourself be seen?"

"She's the one they saw. She's a bit of a klutz." He replied.

"But you're a loner--love'em and leave 'em is your m.o."

Muzzle twitching he agreed, "I would be gone except for them," as two scrawny wild kittens tumbled out of the woods – I present Numb Nuts I and Numb Nuts II"

"Golly" was all I could muster.

"Neither of them will survive this winter without me. She's not a good hunter. She can't teach them to hunt. When they can hunt for themselves I'm gone."

"Well," I teased, "when one thinks cougar one sure doesn't think -oh- a family man!"

To myself I said, "God, I'm talking to a mountain lion."

"Yes, you are," he said twitching his muzzle again.

Then I noticed that like a dog's eyes his held sadness.

Noticing my noticing he said, "There's another. She was caught in a crude trap and found by berry pickers. Since we're endangered in these parts they called the local O.S.P.C.A. One leg was mangled. They tranquilized her. Now, she's ended up in a wildlife preserve with a buffoon of a bear for company. We do get along with bears except at mealtime. In a separate feeding pen, the bear gobbles down his meal. She eats slowly just to drive him wild – so to speak."

In realization, I broke in, "I know her. Oh, so you're the one who visits but they've never seen!"

"And they never will--come summer I'll leave here forever" he said firmly.

202

He looked at me like I was to make it right with her some-how.

Promising I said, "I'll get what food I can for you. How does fish sound because corralling live deer isn't going to happen. " (I already knew that when winter was at its roughest anything would do.)

Putting together loads of fish produced a whole new vision of my life.

Shakily, I got back into my old car and sat warming it. Suddenly all four cats swooshed onto the hood of my car. They rolled around growling in play. The she-lion put her face right up to my side of the windshield and purred, "This is the closest we ever get to a sauna. With winter coming, it is such a treat."

Man, I wanted to idle that car all day. Too soon, they jumped off and were gone. I never saw them again though I knew they watched me.

I headed out thinking to connect with the southbound high-way. Abruptly, I did a u-turn and headed for the Rama Road.

I would go to Hilda. Hilda was my friend and native elder on the Reserve. She wouldn't laugh at me or fear for my sanity. She was wise in the ways of the woods and could give me some answers.

As I flew down Rama Road a memory popped up from my teen years, when I worked in my parents' hardware store. Often stopping into our store, Old Mike from the Reserve counselled my dad on his stock. He would tell Dad how the beavers were building their winter dams. If they were big dams, Dad would double his snow shovel order and we were never under-stocked.

Coming into work, often a stray cat would follow me in the door mewing and purring. Dad accused me of throwing him snacks but I never had.

Mike would smile at me when he heard this. He would say 'kwa anoondwad cog gaan", I would think this was just the mutterings of an old man. Now his words haunted me and I repeated them over and over as I headed for Hilda's.

Once in her driveway, I bounded out of the car, ran up

onto her porch and pounded on her door. It didn't matter if my visit was last week or last year she always welcomed me with open arms. Recognizing my angst she took both my hands in hers. Then, as was her way, she waited quietly.

There was nothing to do but blurt out, "I've just been talking to a cougar family. I was up near..."

Hilda put one hand gently up to my mouth but her words were anything but gentle. "You must never tell anyone where you were. If you are to help them at all you must go it alone. And – they do need your help. They wouldn't have spoken to you if they didn't."

"Oh, Hilda," I sighed, "how can I do this? Please tell me what Mike was saying to me all those years ago. I can't get it out of my head – kwa anoondwad cog gaan."

Eyes twinkling, Hilda said, "He was a wise man. He recognized you even though you didn't recognize yourself. In Ojibway it means "woman-who-hears-the-cats". It is no accident you have all those cats. You must go now. You have a lot of work to do."

Facing my friends was first. It surprised me how easily I found it to skirt around the truth. They asked me if I'd seen the coyote dressed in a cougar's clothing?

"You were right," I lied, "there was nothing to see. My expedition turned out to be shopping in Gravenhurst."

Changing the subject, (but not really) I remarked I would be taking up snowshoeing with my two new knees. I thought 'woman-who-hears-the-cats'. Ha! I would be 'woman-who-haunts-fish-huts' and 'woman-who-smells-like-sardines'. Everyone around me seemed to accept my gathering fish.

"For my cats" I'd say and they just figured my house cats no longer got Fancy Feast.

That winter, every Saturday, I baked banana muffins and made up ham sandwiches while my house cats smiled. Trekking to every fisherman I could find I swapped my food for part of his catch.

Then Sunday, I'd take the fish to Wildcat Woods as I secretly called it. The car drove in as far as it could. With a toboggan loaded with fish, I snow-shoed further and dumped my fish.

Every week when I returned, there wasn't a morsel of fish left. When there hadn't been snow,there were large paw prints. These I covered with snow and unloaded my fresh batch.

By the time the ice was out, I gave up those trips. My wilderness family would now be able to fend for themselves. And I was in better shape than I'd ever been.

Now my only trip that way is to the wildlife sanctuary. I sit on the bench near the maimed she-lion. She had watched me a long time but never talked to me.

Then one late summer day, I silently called across the enclosure, "I knew him too."

She got up and limped towards me. Attempting gracefulness and failing, she flopped down against the fencing near me.

"He's gone now," she said.

"I know." I replied leaning towards her.

Closing time came and I got up to go. When I was several feet away she called out, "Come back sometime."

"Sure," I said and meant it.

§

Notes from a Condemned House

A mind is a terrible thing to waste on housework-Anon.

Many a woman with a full-time job and a full-time family is brought to her knees when it dawns on her that she also has a full-time house. I am a full-time house.

As a house, I have always been content to be in casual shape--very casual shape. My mistress was brought up in "a place for everything and everything in its place" house. She vowed to loosen up when she got her own place and has she ever succeeded! But she has changed. I can feel it all through my faulty wiring. She must have wandered down the cleaning products aisle at No Frills and the smells there must have hit her brain breaking her ties to the " Bingo Babes " and aspiring allegiance to the "Martha Stewart Mamas." Last week she proclaimed, "House. Oh, House! We are going to have a place fit to have a tea party in!"

And I muttered to myself, " as if anyone has tea parties anymore!"

Then she sat down at the kitchen table with a paper and pen. What was she doing? I had to look over her shoulder which really isn't hard when you're the whole house. Truly, I was shocked. She was doing something I'd never seen before. She was making a "To Do" list for getting this place-me-in order.

At the top of the list was-

1: Clean up what you'd be the most embarrassed about someone seeing if they dropped in unexpectedly- like dirty clothes everywhere but in the laundry room. Reminder: Look under the couch.

2: Hide all the books titled "Changing a Boring Sex Life, How to Look Like You're Working or How to Murder Your Neighbour's Dog, Cat or Spouse." She's been doing two for years. That's no accomplishment!

Next she has written-

3: Shine all things that will sparkle especially in the front hall. I know her so well. She thinks people will be so dazzled by the glow, they won't notice the dust on everything else with no shine potential. She's really trying to psych out people with her housekeeping.

She has now written-

4: Have a wastebasket in absolutely every room and keep them all empty even if you have to stash garbage in a bag under the sink or somewhere people won't dream of looking.

Sensing me snooping, she said out loud, "House, if people see all those empty wastebaskets, they'll just assume we hardly make any garbage."

Yeah, right, I feel like responding.

Not to be stopped she listed-

5: Have one or more cats. This really surprises me and she knows it. She assures me you can say things like "that naughty cat brought all those dirty socks into the living room" or "that clever cat leaves dishes at the computer." Just think of the possibilities, House! [Her mother taught her the value of a cat. Her mother's childhood piano teacher would have a full plate of chocolates sitting on the piano, but never offered any to her students. Once when the teacher left for the washroom, her mother had taken a few chocolates, rearranged the plate and then wiped her sticky fingers on the teacher's cat.

"That's fine if, and that's a big if, you can keep the cat from getting into the middle of the living room and cleaning his backside while you have company," I added.

So what's next on her list, I wondered.

6: Make sure Chad has a girlfriend, she ventures as if she can hear me.

"He's only 10!" astounded, I shout back at her.

"Remember when his brother had a girlfriend? Every time his lady-love visited, he vacuumed and washed your floors. If I had known he would do all that for her I would have had him dating much younger."

"I haven't seen you write: One half hour before the guests arrive, stuff all clothes into the spare room and lock the door."

"Thanks a lot, House," she says. (Obviously, I am getting through to her on some level so I keep going.)

"Now, My Dear, sometimes work just has to be done."

"Okay. Okay. I know about this morning when I complained about it being another foggy day and the radio announcer said, 'It's another sunny day in Orillia.' Yes, I'll wash the windows!"

You know, I don't think, as a house, I'll ever be featured in "Better Homes and Gardens "or that Martha Stewart will be calling soon. But then, Martha Stewart ended up in Jail.

MARGOT STRONGITHARM

MARGOT Strongitharm was born in London, Ontario, and spent most of her "learning" years in Chatham and London, where her love of writing was fostered.

She became a teacher of shorthand, typing and business English in Sarnia, then a legal secretary and court reporter for many years in Saskatchewan and Ontario. Later, she was the co-owner/operator of the Midland Dairy Queen restaurant with her husband, Elmer.

Retired and recently widowed, she now lives in a charming cottage on the wooded outskirts of Coldwater, Ontario, where she pursues her interests in quilting, machine knitting, stained glass, cherishing her family and, of course, writing.

Through all the years, she has continued to write, specializing in a style of poetry which she refers to as "life lessons". Margot was the 2010 winner of the First and Third awards for poetry in the Mariposa Writers' Group "Literary Lapses" competition.

Hugs

I like to think the circles in our lives
Will all be hugs -
The kind that clasp and hold us close
And give our hearts a tug.

For hugs are love exemplified -
They make our cares seem less;
They calm and fortify us
When we meet with great distress.

Despite the hardships we endure,
A friend's hug always shows
A strong, unswerving love that dares
To face what fate bestows.

Some heavy trials that we face
Seem more than we can bear;
But each of us will face some test
In life – we'll have our share.

With love and faith, we all can pass
Each test that comes along;
And hugs will go a long, long way
To healing what is wrong.

May all the circles in your lives
Be hugs, to see you through;
Show love by spreading hugs around,
And they'll come back to you.

Ripples

I sat beside a quiet pond,
Its surface smooth as glass;
Like life's unwritten page it lay
In wait for what might pass.

I dropped a tiny pebble in --
It barely made a sound,
But rings of ripples 'round it spread,
And finally ran aground.

I thought about life's circles --
How God drops us on this earth;
The ripples of our influence
Start spreading from our birth.

That day, we cause a tiny splash;
Our circles start to grow --
Then, good or bad, each thing we do
Reflects on those we know.

The ripples that we spread are filled
With opportunity
To touch our families, strangers, friends,
And our community.

Let's all live life in such a way
That, when we meet our end,
We'll be remembered for the good
Our ripples brought to men.

We come from God and go to God,
The circle's then complete;
It's what we do between that counts
Before the two ends meet.

The Easter Lily

A lily lies beneath earth's shroud,
Its glory hid from sight,
Just as our Saviour lay entombed
That day as black as night.

But look! The lily, once thought dead,
Awakes to spring's warm rays,
And now its strong broad blades of green
Push mouldering earth away.

New life that cannot be suppressed
Propels a swelling bud;
Up! Up it reaches – then unfolds
And lifts its face to God.

Its heavenly beauty, unsurpassed,
Defeated dark, dank earth;
And pure and pristine, crisp and clean,
It signifies rebirth.

That seed of life was just as strong
In Christ's breast, where He lay;
The bonds of death could not prevail –
He rose on Easter Day!

His message speaks to all of us
Weighed down by sin and pride,
"Reach up! You, too, can overcome!
It was for you I died."

His promise of eternal life
To those who'll give Him room,
We will remember every time
The Easter lilies bloom.

The Old Oak on the Hill

I'll tell you all a story
About an old oak tree
That grows upon a hilltop
For all around to see.

A hundred years of living
Through storms, drought, sun and rain;
Its gnarled, twisted branches
Show its struggle and its pain.

Its venerable trunk displays
A coat of mossy green
That kept it safe from winter gales –
Where insects now convene.

It's a playground for the chipmunks,
A nursery for birds,
And shade for passing couples
Who've carved on it their words.

So many creatures sheltered –
Its leafy boughs they shared;
Down through the years it held them
With tender, loving care.

In autumn's golden splendour,
Its beauty awes us still;
And 'round its feet the daisies
Dance bright upon the hill.

Where once it shed its acorns,
Oak saplings now grow free;
Its progeny will carry on
When time claims this old tree.

There are lessons for the living
That the oak can tell us all –
Build on strong roots! Care for others!
Persevere whate'er befalls!

VERONICA WELLER

VERONICA was born in Western Canada and when she was 15 years old, her family moved to Ontario. Some years later she moved to Quebec to learn the French language and then off to Europe for a few years. She lived and worked in England and Switzerland before returning to Canada.

Veronica enjoys writing stories for children. This came about after telling stories to her grandchildren and because they loved her storytelling, she decided to write down these stories so as not to forget them, especially since they were asking for repeats.

She and her husband Gunter spend their winters in Mexico where they are able to pursue their hobbies, in particular, bird watching. Each year they are able to add new bird sightings to their life list.

While in Mexico, Veronica does volunteer work with the local pet neutering clinic. The clinic services their village plus three more villages on the Pacific coast north of Puerto Vallarta. The rewards are tremendous because they have seen excellent results in better health for the animals and less stray dogs and cats roaming the local beaches and towns.

A Luncheon Rendezvous

I saw him right away. No mistaking him in the crowd. He is well over six feet tall, slim and walks with a carefree swing, which says he is feeling good and everything in his life is also very good. But then, he always walks tall, bearing a proud, man-about-town air. I think I recognized these traits about him when I first realized just who he was.

The crowd is getting thicker and moving faster. Most of these people only have an hour or less to eat their lunch and try to fit in an errand or two before returning to their offices. I like this crowd even if they are not going far. Somehow it feels exciting. Standing on the corner of 9th Avenue and Palliser Square, Calgary's main downtown crossroads, makes me feel like the world spreads out from this spot like the centre of a giant sunburst.

He's coming closer now. I can see the smile on his face. I would say that he is truly a handsome man. Once I even heard my mother admit that he was very attractive, even downright sexy looking. That's saying a lot from a woman who doesn't like to give an opinion on any subject!

You can tell he is comfortable walking the streets of Calgary. Perhaps that is why he is wearing a Stetson hat. He calls it his ten-gallon hat, the symbol of the stampede city of Canada. Most non-Calgarians would call it a cowboy hat but no true Calgarian would utter such a profane word!

He sees me now. I smile. He lifts his right hand and touches the brim of his stedson hat with the tip of his forefinger, meaning, "I see you too".

All of a sudden he is right in front of me. "Hi honey", he says, "hungry?" "Hi Dad, starving". "Great, let's go to the Palliser Hotel, they serve the best lunch in town".

Go With the Flow

They say one's life should go with the flow,
Does that mean I must accept what I don't know?
Why do we believe these sayings which seem to persist,
When we can just say no and then resist.

To resist the flow means I must have a plan,
Which would say I know what I want and who I am.
I can dream about a lot of things in my own mind,
But to implement a plan really puts me in a bind.

Do I ask others to change their lives just for me,
Fit into my plans and accept whatever will be?
Naturally they will refuse to walk into this great unknown,
Obstacles mount when you won't do things on your own.

I need more than determination and knowledge to get what I need,
As my plans seem to change with every new thing that I read.
Lacking this thing which would make me get up and go,
Makes me back down, give up and just go with the flow!

Scarlett, The Turtle Who Wears Diapers

Chapter I – The Pond Home

I want to tell you about a turtle who wears a diaper. Yes, a real diaper because it does not live in a pond or in a cage but in a house on Bradford Street. Firstly, I should tell you about little Scarlett's life before she came to live on Bradford Street.

Scarlett didn't even have a name back then. She was just a baby turtle in a big pond living with a lot of frogs. All that Scarlett knew about living there was the croaking noises which the frogs made all night long. These noises got so loud that people living on Bradford Street could even hear them!

Scarlett was all alone in the pond with no Mommy or Daddy, only the frogs. So she hid in the pond under some leaves because she was afraid of the frogs. Maybe the frogs were nice and wouldn't hurt Scarlett but she didn't know. All she knew was that their loud croaking noises scared her and she couldn't sleep at night because she didn't know what their noises meant. Was it just noise or was it a warning for people and turtles like herself to stay away from the frogs? With no Mommy or Daddy to tell her, Scarlett was afraid every day.

Then one day when she was still a baby turtle, she heard some strange noises. Not the same noise the frogs made but a deeper noise which sometimes sounded like a swoosh. Whoever was making this noise was also stirring up the water in the pond. Why and what was happening to her pond home? Even if she was afraid of the frogs, it was the only home she ever had and now something was changing it.

Chapter II – Leaving Pond Home

"Give me your stick", called out Braeden. "No", replied Kyle, "get your own stick". So Braeden ran off to the bushes beside the pond and found a suitably long stick just like the one his brother Kyle had picked off the ground. The two boys then began swishing the water in the pond with their sticks. "Can you see any frogs yet?" called out Kyle. "No, I can't see anything because the water is getting really dirty". "OK, let's stop and see if any frogs come up". So both boys stood by the edge of the pond with their long sticks in their hands and waited to see if any frogs would pop up. "Why can't we see any frogs now because we can hear them from home all the time", said Braeden. "I don't know, my friend Jazmine gets frogs out of this pond everyday", replied Kyle. "We will just have to wait a little while and I'm sure they will pop up". "Look over there", pointed Braeden. "What is it? I can't see where you're pointing", said Kyle. "Over on that log, I can see a frog". "No, it's not a frog, it's a little turtle", shouted Kyle. "Let's get it. Get your stick Braeden and pull the log. I'll pull from this end too". Before you could say another word the log started to move and both boys carefully pulled the log with their long sticks because they didn't want the turtle to fall off the log.

"It really is a little turtle, smaller than a frog", said Braeden. "Then it must be a baby turtle, let's take it home", replied Kyle. So Braeden put the little turtle in his pocket and both boys walked home carrying their long sticks.

Chapter III – Where Am I Going

Daddy opened the door to their house as the boys were walking up the steps. "Where have you boys been with those sticks", asked their Daddy. "Over at the pond, we were looking for frogs", replied Kyle. "Well, just remember boys, your Mommy doesn't want any frogs in the house so don't get them out of the pond. Just leave them". Soon it was time for dinner and the whole family sat down at the dining table to eat. Braeden didn't know what to do with the little turtle. Should he leave it in his room? What would happen if the turtle walked out and into the kitchen? No, he thought, I have to keep it in my pocket. When the family was seated around the table their Mommy asked, "So what were you boys doing just now?" "Nothing much", replied Kyle. "They were over at the pond again", said their Daddy. "Just remember boys, don't bring any frogs home because you know I don't want them in the house". "Yes Mommy", they both replied.

"What's the matter Braeden", Daddy asked, "you're

not eating, is something wrong? Are you not well?" "He's OK", said Kyle, "he's just hiding something in his pocket". "No, I'm not", cried out Braeden who was afraid his Mommy and Daddy would discover what was in his pocket and make him take the turtle back."Braeden can tell us about his big secret that's in his pocket", replied Daddy. "It's a turtle", blurted out Braeden. "Well it can't be very big if it's in your pocket. Show us your turtle", asked his Mommy. So Braeden gently picked up the little turtle out of his pocket and put it on the table. The turtle didn't move!

"Braeden, do you know how to care for a turtle. Do you know what to feed a turtle?" asked Daddy. "No", replied both Braeden and Kyle. "You can feed the turtle Mommy when we are at school", suggested Kyle. "No, that will not happen", she said. "You have two choices. One is to return the turtle to the pond and the second choice is to find it a good home. The choice is up to you boys". Kyle and Braeden looked at each other and they both knew that they didn't want to take the turtle back to the pond. "Why can't we give the turtle to Mr. and Mrs. Mark, they don't have any pets", said Kyle. "Yes", said Braeden, "then we can go to see the turtle everyday at their house". So it was decided that after dinner Kyle and Braeden would go to their neighbours to see if they would be willing to adopt their turtle.

Chapter IV – Finding A New Home

Happily Mr. and Mrs. Mark agreed to adopt Kyle and Braeden's turtle and to give it a good home. Come to visit us anytime was the invitation given to the boys.

"Oh my, did you ever imagine having a turtle as a pet", Mrs. Mark asked her husband. "No, never but now we have to learn how to care for it", he replied. "Well", said Mrs. Mark, "if we're to have a pet in the house the first thing it needs is it own name". "But we don't know if it's a boy or a girl", said Mr. Mark. "It doesn't really matter because I think it would be fun to think of the turtle as a little girl. I have always loved the name Scarlett. What do you think?" "I agree", replied her husband, "let's name her Scarlett". So that is how she came to be called Scarlett.

Scarlett's life now became very different from her first

home in the pond at the very end of Bradford Street. Scarlett still lives on Bradford Street but now in a nice home with new parents who have promised to be very nice to Scarlett.

Mr. Mark decided that he must go to the pet store right away and buy some food for Scarlett because they didn't know what she could eat nor how often they should feed her. Is once a day enough or is twice a day even better? Can she sleep on a blanket or must they buy a log? Do they need lots of water for Scarlett to live in or will a cage be just as good? When Scarlett needs to go to the toilet, would a litter box be good? After all, cats use litter boxes so why not a turtle too?

Oh my, so many questions! They were hoping they could get all the answers at the pet store. "Well", said Mr. Mark when he returned from the pet store, "they could not answer my questions but they did have some turtle food which I bought". "That's the most important thing", said his wife, "but what else did you buy?" "I bought a kitty litter box, a small cage and a little blanket to put in the cage. Do you think she will sleep in a cage?" "I don't know, but we can try to see how she likes it even if it's just for one night. Let's go to bed now and see what happens with Scarlett tomorrow".

Chapter V – Scarlett's First Day In Her New Home

In the morning when Mr. and Mrs. Mark got up from their bed, they saw that Scarlett had not slept in the cage, had not eaten her food but rather she left a mess on the floor for them to clean up. "Well, that settles it, Scarlett must wear a diaper", said Mr. Mark. So, Mrs. Mark cut up some cloths to make tiny diapers for Scarlett.

"What are they doing to me?" wondered Scarlett to herself. "They have turned me over on my back and put something on me. How can I go to the toilet with this thing around me? Do they expect me to just go to the toilet anyway? Oh my, how many times are they going to do this to me?"

They keep saying Scarlett, Scarlett, come here! That must be my name because I hear that word all day long. Mr. Mark always picks me up and I can sit beside him on the sofa. Sometimes he puts me on his lap when he is reading his book. Now that I've lived here for a few days I find the food is not too bad after I've tried it a few times but I will not sleep in that big awful cage they got for me. I like open spaces better. Finally they have put a soft cloth down on the floor for me and I can sleep there. Do you know what I like about my new home? There are no more frogs to scare me and best of all I love sleeping in Mr. Mark's lap! It is so comfortable and warm and quiet, just what I have always wanted. At last I have the best home for me! So when those boys come here for a visit, I will let them pick me up. I will not hide under my blanket because they were really nice to me and they found me a new home.

Chapter VI – All About Turtles

Turtles help clean rivers and lakes. They live where they can find the right food, shelter and temperature.

Some Common Questions About Turtles

1.   Why do turtles bask (lay) in the sun in summertime?

This is because they are reptiles and cannot make their own heat. The sun helps raise their body temperature up to between 16 and 35 degrees Celsius so that they can digest their food better. Also, their muscles work better if they are warm.

2.   Do turtles have a good sense of smell?

Yes, they use their smell to identify food, mates, territory, etc. On land, turtles smell things the way we do. Under water many have special little bumps that contain a sense of smell on their chins to help them find food in the dark or muddy water. Tiny Painted Turtles are born knowing the smell of a Snapping Turtle which means danger and they can dive for cover quickly.

3.   Do turtles see well?

Yes. They even have colour vision, particularly red. They can detect small differences in pattern and shape. This means they recognize their own species and avoid enemies. Turtles see only what is in front of them.

4.   Do turtles hear well?

No. They do not have an ear drum but they can detect low frequency sounds and pickup vibrations on land and in water.

5.   Can turtles carry diseases?

Yes. They can carry Salmonella and can suffer from it too, especially in polluted waters. Very small children should not touch turtles in the wild. Wash hands very carefully.

6.   Why do turtles cross roads and highways?

Mostly it is the adult female who crosses in the nesting season and she is trying to find a warm sunny place to bury her eggs. They need southern exposure with more direct sun, appropriate soil humidity and little or no plant cover. Female turtles may use these good sites for generations.

7.   What should we do if a turtle is crossing the road?

Help it in the direction it is already going. Very small turtles can be lifted but be careful as they have claws and sharp beaks. Try sliding the turtle onto a shovel, a piece of cardboard or plywood by its tail but do not do this to a large turtle because you would break its tail.

8.   Is it true that the turtle's shell is very hard?

No. The shell is quite thin and easily crushed.

9.   How many different turtles are there in Canada? There are 9.

(a)   Western Painted Turtle

(b)   Midland Painted Turtle

(c)   Common Snapping Turtle

(d)   Wood Turtle

(e)   Spotted Turtle

(f)   Blanding's Turtle

(g)   Common Musk Turtle

(h)   Eastern Spiny Softshell Turtle

(i)   Common Map Turtle

        Website: Turtle S.H.E.L.L. Tortue

JANKE WIELENGA

JANKE is a poet presently living in Orillia, Canada. A transient in search of a home, born in the Netherlands, she immigrated to Canada in the 1950s with her family at age three and by age six had moved across Southern Ontario: Aylmer, Kirkton, Kippen, and Clandeboye. Over the years, the moves continued: Hensall, Farquer, Drayton, Kitchener, Listowel, Waterloo, Thunder Bay, Paris, and Orillia.

Transience of careers and education matched the moves: farm worker, room attendant, homemaker, host, dental assistant, receptionist, teacher, librarian, bookseller, researcher, writer with B.A. in English and M.A. in Religion, Poetry & Story. Some of her poems have won awards and been published in various anthologies and magazines, including *Women & Environment International Magazine, Open Minds Quarterly, Exclamations In Ink, Cranberry Tree Press, Canadian Stories, and Freefall.*

something simple

there's something
so simple
about green maple leaves
in my window
the silence of their trust
the simple beauty
of their open hands
calling me to sing the simple
breath of wind's love
that kind of open melody
and courage to be
alive green gracious brief
and open to the hands
of summer's moment
summer's yes
as easily as the lift and fall
of leaves
my heartbeat just a moment
in the envelope of time's
gift before the orange
crescent the red slash
and yellow banner
of autumn's death call
settles in my chest
and the falling into
love begins

Present

When she came in carrying
a little jug of summer flowers
in the palm of her hand,
the room shifted
to accomodate the shiver,
the flowers tousled,
sleepy almost
tucked in their little nest
of water in a jug,
such haphazard cluster,
'these are for you' she said
her presence suddenly present,
the sun a golden puddle in
the feverfew,
two sprigs of lavender
purple as a feast,
and eager knotweed
teasing gentle queen anne's lace,
and other little purple playthings,
everything smelled softly,
the clover sweetness of summer
came in with her - fields glistening
in the sun, bees busy brushing love
inside the small faces of field flowers.

Chickadee Theories

Oh who can catch the chickadee?
no summer wind or sun or rain can daunt

the debutante arrangement of this bird
its feathers soft as wistful down, as fawn

as silk its bum, in handfuls tossed through
sunshine's hip hop flop and do not stop

the world is heavy shrug it off - fly
and raven's droop, that black blue silken burden

of body unbearable to feed and preen
that mute dumb caw will not bear you away

joy can sit and twirl on sticks in the spireas
the potintilla and quiver it where raven

never comes to sit because the sticks
would break and raven tumble down

move fast past pockets of dead bird breath
and baby ravens treat with nimble illusion

let them have the worms with their noses
in the grasses like cows in pasture pecking

travel light and talk to strangers only in absence
of stationary treasure - be self contained

like a drop of water sip often and fly
with confidence and abandonment

life's only a bundle of feathers and blood
packed in dust

april circuit of strings and cat baskets.

the chickadees are tying strings in the pontintilla
unravelling threads in sprockets and spools
trading secrets between them handily
lighthearted flounders and pinwheels
twirls in a gig to startle the cat
she's come to prowl and slink beneath them
belly brushing earth head turned up sniffing
and the chickadees laugh sponge fest
tease that cat dip low nosedive and swoop
tying the threads in bunches straw as slender
as fragile as a nest in little pieces
tied together with the brown tranquility of twigs
and cat scoundrel slinking
speckled orange black and yellow
bright as a canary no catch
these bird brown bumps in the bushes
teetering on the round white rim
and dipping in tipped down for a sip of water
dip and fly another mission between the purple lilac
and the spirea bush and hop
the last fall's leaves and grasses
garden's dried shred's and sticks a feast of nesting
sunflowers hollow eyed empty sockets
all seeds gone to chickadee bellies
for the winter feeding and this
april circuit of strings and cat baskets
stooped to conquer cat
swivel her dizzy with little bird
minuets

Episode With Birds

This morning the sky's milky, a cow's udder,
birds crazy in their invisible mapping
fly handfuls of various blood-beats,
hearts in motion, wing spanned,
carried over and back, this travel
this morning in March
ten degrees and melting,
the arrangement of music
is magnificent, my eyes mark time
and watch the performance.

Crows black night spots herald
secrets, their nest they bless with open
wings and hovering, then settle down
down inside the hidden tuft of pine top –
just the right broom bottom bush
to cover and sway musically
on heaven's array and stay safe,
murmur with wind's love and abrasion.

Seagulls single in several tiers
like pale milkpails blend
and subtly bring the sea
over lazily loft, the little birds
scamper and fret, their wings tadpoles
and harrows, they paddle and lilt,
they cavort and tilt like a plough
in the tune of its furrow.

The sky is a mess of bird
happiness and the morning's
in tune with the sun that peeks
out just to see the bird legs
abound and string busy
ties in every bare branch,
every ounce of new spring
air inhaling - this is the
flounce, the busy bounce
and percussion of bird habitat.

Oh where do they hide
in the winter's backside
to so loop and leap
this milky morning in March?

§

Kissing Your Two Lips

Purple petals, six scalloped
passions in a cup, six purple stamens
clustered around the pale yellow pistil
the colour of skin
in the yogurt container with Source
written on its side in dark navy letters
on a slant, the S like a swivel
of chickadee wing.

When I open the blossoms
it's a feast of lines and brackets
an explosion of purple tranquil
tulip
purple stamins stand up like frozen mittens
little sabers
the cluster of six stamins round the erect
pistil and round the stamins the six
purple petals so nicely scalloped
like the cluster of chickadees
on the rim of the sour cherry pail
in the center of garden trash.

The purple tulips reign
a royal handful
five fingers held out regally
with just that poise
of Queen Elizabeth's hand
in a parade extended - practised
yet delicate
never seeming to tire out
succulent enough to touch
to brush my nose inside the cusp
of petals and come out purple
breathing dusty kisses
fields of flowers
chickadees dipping down
for a sip of water
sitting on a load of hay
in summer laughing
in the rumple of purple dust.

All Summer She Brought in Flowers

bachelor buttons dressed for church
sins covered hands washed arranged significantly small

whiter than snow my father sang Sundays after church
the milk cans returned from Stacey Bros our reward

for hand milking sixty cows morning evening always
cows patient as her hand tending flowers

in her summer garden standing still
our hands curled teats and took the milk

this week she brought in three calendula suns
tousled mops a comfort for hands to riffle through

feel the soft tether stain, that laughter one wants
to remember to arrange concerts to celebrate breathing

we learn from summer flowers milkweeds
paths worn hard by cows walking following the manner

of weaving chewing cud taking time to catch
blossoms waver repeat see sleep and cherish waking

we stay and thank full she talks about her flowers
every day in petals little bursts of admiration signs

calendula spray rejoice fear time ticks and walks
the petunias spread their purple baskets

catching teacups in their black cool centers
love is hard to hoe weeds want to scruff it out

take over blur the lines and feed on ecstasy forgotten
so much money takes to live to let the day content

its clock hands walking off again and leaving us behind
stolen hours of sleep in evening's gift come in for payment eyes

socketed and sunken worry broods and tethers
the horses stamped and nuzzled noses soft as moss

and welcome to the hands to calendula laugh and sleep

gather dreams wash the morning roof lines with belief and belief and...

§

October Morning

The burning has begun, night frost ripped black the stems,
the daisies in their window box *bedrooft*, astonished,
robbed of their carefree charisma, yellow ears pulled back
all nose now, and blinking cross-eyed,
totally deranged from summer's toss and float
bumblebee whirring kiss me sort of faces,
perfect love me whumped to love me not
in one raw night. They had me
believing they would last forever.

The dahlia is dead, it bloomed late august royal
purple soft in shadow of the lilac, sloped under in
demeanor of down.

The marigolds still stand in strand, ripped soldiers,
burned orange spit, dribbles of blooms stuck on top,
riffled Van Goghs finally claiming their painting.

The sunflowers hunch like women draped in gloom,
faces bowed inside collars, licking leaves broad as men's hands,
like lamp shades, shutting out the surface,
one has its face in the marigolds, its few scraps of tendrils
tickling the shrivels of orange cusp.

Only the alyssium still queen in the garden borders
with their snow flakes in the hands of children,
and the petunia has a new bugle
at bottom of the window box;
a few white blossoms
the size of thumbprints peek out.

The robin is a complete surprise,
strutting father perfect with his faded breast
a dusty orange.

(*bedrooft*-- dutch for sorrowful, bereaved)

after the leaves fall

before the snow arrives to pull the wool
over our eyes in mid december
the light ducks its head
brushes everything with dusk
the air askance with wood
 the color of barn doors
a thousand thousand little sticks stand out
 and up on tiptoe
to catch the basket of sun that blooms
 from ten to four and then blinks out
a switch shut off
the wheelbarrow's tipped up
like a tea cup
 resting from summer labour
empty of mud and leaves
against the bench where in july
basins of peas and potatoes
fresh from the garden waited washing
everything's twine
 spoors and tracks of spider webbed trees
with black handles for arms
and spigots for fingers
 green gowns gone
only naked bones
click in the somnambulant wind
the flag on hillcrest park
slouches like a lazy farmer
after sunday brunch

Evergreen in Snow Storm

The way the snow licks your fingertips
like icing to tongue, lovingly laid flake
by flake, as though to dress your needlepoint
were an exquisite gesture of fulfillment
in some measure of weather harvest.
Snow iced lightly white needle crystals
sunday dressed so quickly in the snow
falls cocoon like honey in a jar, sugar
canes like finger food for children sucking
mittens snow meshed, with red cheeks
and snotty noses, laughing. Your laughter
in this sudden arrangement of white wedding
fingerpoint in your deeply green veined
spine space silently spills out in ribs of
scattered blooms, tulips just about
to sprout red yellow blue and purple
petals and the daffodils dog eared
with perfect poise and smell of horses
farting are jealous of your majesty
so easily bride swept for snow swept
harvest. Spring spatula performed
between the acts of flower poise,
white noise that chuckles
in the beds of March.

January Praise Psalm

The snow pearls, draws breathing
across the windows, feasts the trees,
everything tied together with
pearling flakes - this abiding moment.

Oh who can win this carnival of snow,
its obedience to God is amazing–
falls and falls in luscious devotion,
cavorting like children in play tumble
and lick mittens.

The pine tree, that crooked haggard
monster in my window frame,
slaps its crooked wings against the wind,
flapping for flight, marooned on its stem,
oh far the finger-nimbled pine
sticks its fingers in the sky,
breathtaking views of nimble
assembly - forgiveness for our sins.

And in the night we lie with the moon
coming in the window,
wrapped in the veil of each other's skin,
the snow racing its death watch,
laughing in anxious hurry to fall
cavorting to the grave in minions
of starbursts.

Across the street the little house
of Hansel and Gretel is covered
in white candy, the dunes of its roof
ski slopes, prayer . . . our Father, our Mother.

Surely we know death now,
just to look outside is to smell the dust–
maybe we'll finally understand snow
when we sleep that last sleep.

Oh come and play on the roof below,
the little white house has a field of snow
on its head, we'll play fox and geese
and catch me if you can.

§

Winter Ravens in Snowfall

Two ravens in the brawl
of winter's tree, preening
and cleaning themselves,
unwrapping black robes,
wings pumping air,
heads bobbing
like old pumps, pruning
a raucous kaw kaw,
and a quack.

Hooded outlaws,
blue black silhouettes
comforting containment
like two chickens perched
side by side,
two full black jugs.

The snow falls,
a tree lined skin scape,
little birds fleeting
and cheeping,
carrying snow dust
from branch to branch,
the trees fuzzy, snow soft.

Shaking off
the dusty invasion
the ravens lift off,
their wingspan airplane,
finely tuned
to the flag's swallow
high up on Hillcrest Park.

Snow like chop dust
shuffles past my window.
Now I lay me down
to sleep,
the snow daylight
falls little.

Before The News At Six

So between attention the November night gathers black and brilliant
tied up strings of twigs and legs stuck out in all directions
walking air and lingering around to lick the shadows once again
as light bleeds into dusk.

So we transport the day with our few groceries,
walking home from work or school and touching tree trunks
with our hands and feet crushing leaves,
the rustle dry and friendly to our footfalls.

So our shoes walk in air with loveliness for meeting places
pathways like a trail for lives that travel back and forth
between days, and everything in twilight,
all the broken promises that hurry home
and shut the door behind them,
and you, tree, have lost so much again,
a family of leaves in thousands dropped and shot,
crushed under foot armies of leaves,
your bare black bones as beautiful as silhouettes,
a smash of living, holding out arms, hands and finger tips
to touch the furthest tongue tips air,
nodules already nibbling into bud birth.

So much feathertip and black storage, rooms to dress up in,
whiskers, brush strokes, life before the news at six
begins to shut us in with bits of information,
a house fire that burns a family up,
nine heartbeats rearranged to hide,
inside the folding wings of ravens,
sitting like black trophies in the crooked scaffolding
the twilight holds with easy arrangement.

So blue bleak light gives forgiveness for the missing welcome,
windows full of light and pictures facing out, no visitors,
the empty basket of twilight gathers so much belief
to hold on for resting through the night,
we find our sustenance in skin and bones
and listening to the maples naked succulence
to bring us home.

§

Meningitis

The weight of her walking home
from school at noon
the first day of spring
she fourteen and I eleven
carrying those acres
of snow in her head packed
like a snowfort with whacks
and thumps hammered in
with mittens
the freezing searing in her eyes
the snow bulging - and no
yellow daffodils anywhere
no searing red
tulips or purple lilacs
crying to be let out yet
only this snow forever
crammed inside her head
like this her eyes two shovels
of coal burning in the pale
linen of her face undressed.

She slept the sleep of the dead.

O Death, Where is Thy Sting?

(To My Father a Week after his Burial)

So now so suddenly you're shut up
your voice, your face, that red rooster hair
and those beef master hands, shut up
inside the snow here somewhere, buried.
All I see is a dome of soft soft snow,
the shape of a dead cow when it
fell, bloated from too much clover.
Wind sculpts little shrouds of sleeping
children in among the tombstones,
but your plot has no stone just this dome.

So now you can't catch me anymore
when I'm hiding from you on the telephone
and you're calling with that scowling hello
that sends me scuttling back and forth
with false friendliness and stretchmarks
on the walls. You believed hymns and
sang them gustily to the presence of
anyone else's peace of mind.
Whiter than snow, yes whiter than snow
now wash me and I shall be whiter than snow.

The blue dog wails and whines for you to walk
the lane to the barn but the snow has washed
you away. Your rubber boots lie folded
two praying hands you flopped off the last
night after chores. Your barn cap stranded
with straw and spiders you kicked in the corner
by your chair. It sits staring emptily across the table.
Mother's eyes are broken, the blue is spilling over
and my hands can't catch it. She limps to the kitchen,
the kettle's whistling for tea.

A Room in February Lamplight

Alone now, he is dead.
The house is February snow and snow wind.
She is listening, time belongs nowhere.

In the late February snow she is alone inside
her wooden log house out in the country.

The dusk to dawn lamp burning on its pole,
lights house, pine trees, dunes and hollows,

fields of snow with shadows in the peaceful glow
of the company of light. She is sitting in the den,

Now he is dead and she is Widow,
left stranded like a broken shoe kicked off
and shoved away inside this closet space,

a dusky room held close by walls and doors
with a window looking out into the lamplight

holding the pines carefully together safely.
She sits and reads, the house quiet with itself

and herself, the logs holding her together
inside this room this winter this February.

forgotten, passed by his passing on.
bereft, cut off inside this house of logs
her husband loved and built for their retirement.

His presence still lingers in fleeting glimpses,
shreds of thought, a mouse scratching its tiny feet

on the backside of a log, the shush of the furnace
catching, the lamplight burnishing the shadows

holding the night in its arms. In this room he lay
down in September with lawns still green with lust

Widow is a word that flies around the beams
like blind bats that swoop out of the chimney's crack,
he slew with the tennis racket when he was living.

holding the house, and the chickadees hopping
and feeding, fat healthy blood, laughing handfuls

in the windowsills. And he could stay no longer,
no time to relish the harvest of the fields

of corn and the birds flying away for winter,
the snow building its strange scallops undulating

here he met death and lay
two weeks waiting death and she with him
inside this room day and night unto the death.

porch, lawn, and laneway, acres and acres of full white.
The silence of his death she holds inside herself

as dusk to dawn the lamp binds earth to sky, snow
to light, pine to wind, log to house, intimately.

The widow knows, the widow
weeps, the widow waits inside
the dusky light of grief.

The Stupor of Mourning

summer saturdays at seven
just before the sun gathers up its going down
my sister cuts a handful of pink carnations
from her flower garden and drives to town
turns left at the light   a short distance   to the cemetery
she walks across to where he lies
beneath a spindling evergreen beside a fence
beside a field   beside a river

she built him a stone like the dodge ram
he washed with so much love on saturdays

with dustcloth stuffed beneath her car seat
she sweeps away the lawn mowers spray and bird flight
tears of stain and blame
his monument   a black mirror of silence
and the dusk climbs up the hill on the other side
coming up from the river taking the pine tree along in its face
the fence a comfort between

and she bends to lay her handful down
memory   his black ford coupe 1956   white sport coat
a pink carnation

love me tender carved in stone

Dusk's Litany

Every evening in winter, as the blue bleak takes day away,
we are walking again that journey home from school,

my sister and myself, in the snow-tombed roads, the whiteness
like a furnace in our faces, burning hands and feet, red

and searing, sliding shut the day, light slowing with each step.
The barnboard trees, all ragged mops, spine fingered, sliced

with snow falling, falling now, leak out into the smear
of black paint, the dusk easing into this still that sits inside

the album in my head like stranded lilacs in their winter dress
and all the sticks as naked as our souls, stripped of their daylight.

Our mother is dead and we are walking home from the one room
school house S. S. No 5 Hay Township. It's almost Christmas

and the bus cannot come, the roads too full of drifts and photographs
of snow. Our three brothers have run ahead, plunging through

the drifts as though their feet were glass and they the skaters
in a feast of ice snow. But my sister has my hand to hold her down,

she is thirteen and I am six, my feet are half the size of hers,
her legs can swallow up three times mine, so I'm hopping

like a chickadee between the steps, and running snot out of my nose
for comfort, and the dusk is eating everything inside a blue heaven,

our mother is somewhere out there now inside the black horizon,
between the window and the school and the road that's broken down

with snow, the journey takes a lifetime, and replays its frozen fingers

like an overture to so much bewilderment, her cancer slicing out our
hearts

and tongues, our eyes darkness, the living room a cardboard cutout
with sticks figures moving arms and legs like pendulums, clocks

striking the hour, empty is a feeling only dusk understands.

§

The Room

To this room, just a corner in Clandeboye,
my mother, pioneer of so much travel, retired.
Wrapped in gauze and gingerale she communed
with Jesus and pain that ripped her mouth
until Nurse Faber came with her white shoes,
her needle and the blessed morphine,
till Jesus lulled her fear, promising one final move,
just one more gathering of her self, her face
and hands body skin hair soul, and then rest.

The door is shut the door is shut do not go in
Your mother lies inside the door with bandages

around her breasts do not go in do not go in
the door is shut the door is shut. Come hide

beneath the table now where no one else can see
you watching for nurse Nell to come

with shoelaces tight, her shoes so white,
her walk so right, straight to your mother's door.

And if you lie down very flat upon the carpet bare
its roses red and stained with petals bleeding

in your head, then you can peer out just beneath
the tablecloth's deep fringe and see her turn the knob

and pull the door ahead, in that glimpse of open before
she steps inside your mother's face you'll see

upon the pillow and you can burn her with your
eyes and visit her inside your head and murmur

count and murmur mama mama mama your heart
a boom box in your chest, your hands two lumps of coal

your mother's face is like a ghost, it has no light,
it has no shine, her skin is white, her lips are closed.

The door is shut the door is shut do not go in.

§

Afternoons to Tea

It seems that I have always known her touch,
surrounded by the apron of her skin,
her round allure like black potbellied stove
red hot and smoking in the center room.

She sewed alone with me on winter days
and let me play with button troves in honey pails.
I'd scatter them like horses in a field,
or cluster them like daisies in a garden plot.

And she would tell me how her life had changed
since coming to this land of frozen bones,
her children walking miles without warm boots,
her husband keeping water bottles hot
beneath his shirt while working in the barn.

We'd drink our tea together in the sun
and she would say to me, "Come, kissie face,"
her voice the taste of old-banana bread,
"you need to eat a bit to make you grow."

I thrived those timeless winter afternoons,
before the others tumbled in the door
with red-puffed faces, snow-specked coats,
and mittens eager for the sizzling stove.

Until one silver day at the end of June,
my mother went to Jesus, or so they said,
and never traveled back to sew with me,
to drink warm tea and keep me company.

The clapboard house became a summer waste
where wind whistled dirt through window cracks,
and shadows waved her face from memory.
But mourning has the setting stuck for me
in winter's storm with mother's stove gone cold.

Water Closet

My father believed in purifying tendencies
stranger to bathtubs   fearful of soap's itch
he sang lustily *now wash me and I shall be whiter than snow*

Our bathtub was a resting place for flies
that died and tumbled in   out of the windowsill
after trekking up and down the pane
as patiently as Sisyphus with his stone

We never questioned
that the bathtub on its claws   obese as any mother sow
stay dry   plugged shut   to keep flies from dropping
down the drain   dust balls comforting the dying

Just once my brother filled the tub
with his long underwear soaked with mustard plaster
he'd applied to suffocate his chest
and smother winter's cough

But no   we never bathed
water was too valuable   for that frivolity and splash
a miracle to hoard   like loaves and fishes
the faith that wobbled my father and stepmother

We never asked why water was so hard to find
the flushing toilet cringed   its rush a waterfall marked shame
the pipe ran through the kitchen closet
what a waste   cows nuzzle water like velvet teacups
lick and shower   saliva flies and tails flick

Water cost so much   confusion   listen
the counting gravel rushes down the pipes
cringe before the law marked   father
hide inside the calendar marked   mother

sleeping in her yellow bed with her own bandages
her own pain crooning a pathway in her head
showing her the way to jesus

escape is longing to be empty
of these things we gather and store to shore us up
dust lives happily ever after
if we could just arrange to listen to its lullaby

This morning the water lies in dunes
the tub wipes its windshield on my toes

§

The Way We Left Her There

Her life we stole from her with bottles full of bible texts
half a dutch milk chocolate bar with coffee and whipped cream

sundays after church   too many calendars   her father dealt
in live stock   dread   John Calvin knew her father well

she sent along black bananas   cardboard boxes full
banana bread sliced   kitchen table   tea   the Family Herald

tears   mending in her lap   fingers counting threads
patches of longing   her life   made up of holes

to fill and fix   stuff full of threads   wool darning
shutting up the open mouths of death's bite

her life a daily testament   to three brothers strapped
to stall and field sweating straw and insulage

hay chewing holes for her to fill with tears and wool
the drunken car had broken through so rudely   ripped

her own three little ones   sent them tumbling on ahead
into eternity to watch her toiling with all those holes

she that hides in the secret place
of the most high shall abide
under the shadow of the almighty

we fed her peanut butter cookies that last evening
before her operation   her kidneys failed

oh how we wished we'd come in time to help her
with tomato soup   we kissed her lips and left

she arranged herself scantily enough   journal   kleenex
telephone   her bedside table

please don't leave anything behind
the cookie crumbs we brushed away

-one step between ...

the way we sang   *when peace like a river* and plucked
the orange roses out of the spray on her coffin

and the funeral director bending over   her skirt a black hollow
beckoning the children to come   see the cement vault

and *her* lying inside the oak coffin balanced on golden spindles
poised like a dancer for the final drop   the final hole

the way we left her there alone   and walked away
as always   in a graveyard stones comfort stones

her stone unwashed   we tried to look the other way
no one thought to wash it down before the funeral

her name already there   waiting for her arrival

TAMMY WOODROW

TAMMY was born in Montreal to Lorna Olsen and James Walter Dore. A long-time Oro-Medonte resident, Tammy currently lives in Moonstone with her husband and two daughters.

Creativity is a dominant trait of Tammy's. She has explored several different creative avenues from wall murals to oil paintings to writing, to name a few. As a child, she was hardly ever found without crayons and paper in her hands.

Now, as an author/illustrator of children's books, Tammy has found a direction that is both exciting and rewarding. *Bellus Terra* is her first novel which was published in 2010 by Pine Lake Books. More recently, *Sunny Honebee Is Lost* is her first picture book.

Filled with ideas and dreams, Tammy is looking forward to a long and successful career in making children and their parents laugh and enjoy.

Chapter One
(From the Novel entitled "Painted Dreams")

Saying Goodbye was never easy. It had been almost three months since Leigh's grandmother had passed away and her dreams grew more and more detailed. Opening her tired eyes, Leigh raised heavy hands and rubbed her lids as she wiped a tear away. It wasn't that her dreams were bad; in fact it was just the opposite. They would always start as different settings and in one way or another she would end up over and over again on her Gramma's front porch using 'the natural light' to paint the same oil painting, while Gramma Kate would paint another. The two were 'kindred souls' Gramma would say as she smiled her beautiful smile.

For a child that was the youngest of three, Leigh received more attention in this crafty old house with her Gramma than any-where else. She dropped by as often as she wanted. Laughing again over milk and cookies Leigh and Gramma Kate compared their artistic versions of the garden with its statues and flowers. Gramma's paint-ings were always perfect in Leigh's mind while hers she felt were silly blobs of colours not always where they were supposed to be. "In time my Dear," Gramma would say. "I have been painting for years you are just learning the feel of the brush," she would add as she kissed the top of Leigh's head and squeezed her shoulders. It never mattered what Leigh's finished painting would be Gramma would pick it up and hang it somewhere in the house. "You'll be famous one day and I want to have as many as I can before the rest of the world will want them," she would say with such assurance.

Always just before she would wake up, Leigh would fol-low her Gramma into her living room and find herself staring at a painting of a beautiful gravel laneway lined with trees of the most amazing fall colors, and that was how it would end. Knowing that her Gramma never had a painting like that in her living room or any room in her house for that matter she assumed that it represented the fact that Gramma Kate had passed away in the fall. October was Gramma Kate's favourite month of the year and so it held many memories for Leigh, new and old. Gramma Kate's birthday was in October and so had Grampa Dean's been. They had been married the first of October and so it was a very special and happy time. They were very young when they met and very much in love. Leigh remembered that Grampa Dean would say that he knew he would marry Gramma Kate from the first time he saw her pretty face and beautiful eyes. They had three children of their own and Leigh was the only daughter of their youngest son Mark. Grampa had passed away only two years ago and even though Gramma was happy most of the time Leigh knew she missed him terribly and wanted to be there for her. All that was gone now and even though Gramma Kate was okay with her time coming to an end it was still Leigh that was left behind, alone and without her best friend.

Sitting up, Leigh looked to her side table and wiped at another tear as she gazed at the present her Gramma had given her for her fifteenth birthday, just five months ago. It was a top of the line art set with flat brushes, round brushes, fan brushes and oil paints of all colors. "Never stop painting my Dear, it's what your eyes really see!" The clock read 7:33 and even though it was Saturday morning it was still time to get up. If her Dad and brothers hadn't left already for hockey they soon would be running out the door and that meant that Leigh would have at least an hour with her Mom before she too would have to go to the arena. With older brothers so devoted and crazy for hockey both parents needed to be chauffeurs as well as fundraisers to help with the costs of the all the fee's and equipment. It didn't help either that both brothers had to be goalie's, which only added to the price. They were very good though and Leigh would often go to their games to cheer them on. Unfortunately she was not as gifted in the athletic department and so most of her time was spent on the sidelines in many ways. Standing up and stretching her growing limbs out Leigh shuffled her way down the hall and into the kitchen where her mother was making some toast. As she turned the corner her Mom chuckled to herself and wished her bed-headed daughter a good morning.

"Even with your hair in all directions and those worn out fleece pyjamas you still make the most beautiful entrance a girl could," she praised. "Now what'll it be?" She asked as she leaned against the counter.

"Just some toast this morning," Leigh replied as she yawned widely.

"You still look very tired," Jacqueline frowned. "Are you sleeping alright?" Knowing how close her daughter had been with her mother-in-law Jacqueline worried that her baby was still grieving a great deal. Always quieter than her two boys, her daughter seemed even more distant than before Kate's passing and the last four months had been very difficult for her.

"Just tired, I don't feel like I'm getting a lot of sleep even though I know I am," Leigh shrugged. "It's probably just all the school work that's been dumped on us lately, it always gets heavier just before Christmas holidays," Leigh added as an after-thought.

"Okay then, one order of toast coming up," Jacqueline said as she grabbed the loaf of bread from the counter and twisted the plastic tag off the end to open the loaf. Pulling out two slices of bread and dropping them into the slots, she punched the toaster knob down and was spinning the loaf of bread expertly to snap on the tag as she turned to say, "I have to go to the arena again and cover the snack bar you wanna come?"

"No that's okay Mom. I have to work on a paper for Tuesday and I might as well get a good chunk of it done today while the house is quiet. But thanks," replied Leigh as she waited for the toast she could now smell.

"Alright, you know the number and I'm only a few blocks away. If you need anything, just call. I'll bring home some lunch," her Mom nodded and turned again to pull the toast from the toaster and place them on a small plate. Knowing full well that Leigh only ate peanut butter on her toast, she pulled a butter knife from the drawer and slid the jar of p.b. across the island to where Leigh sat grinning. In the next moment her mother drank the last of her coffee and was heading for the shower. Nothing tasted better with peanut butter toast than a tall cold glass of milk and Leigh headed straight for the cupboard to get a glass. It was going to be a long, quiet morning and she wanted to get started so she filled her glass and just as quickly tipped it up and drank it down in steady gulps until it was done. Folding her toast in half she walked back to her room eating as she went.

The afternoon passed as quickly as the morning unfortunately had and now the house was filled with voices both on the television and around the house. Leigh's brothers Dan and Mitch had come back from their games with some of their friends and they were arguing about a play that a Toronto Maple Leaf had made that was penalized. It sounded like the fight would be in her living room as well as on the ice. Jacqueline was just getting involved when Mark entered the room and told the boys to shape up or ship out. The living room was not a place that Leigh was interested in being right then. As had happened a few times in the past two months Leigh began to walk to the closet to grab her coat and head to Gramma's when she remembered that that plan wasn't going to work. Shaking off the pain she decided to go for a walk anyways and see how much snow was on the ground in the small town of Stonewater. Grabbing her thick winter coat from a hanger and wrapping a scarf around her neck Leigh tugged on her winter boots and headed out the front door. She found herself walking towards her Gramma's house anyways even though it had been sold recently and her mother told her it wouldn't hurt as much if she just let some time pass before going by it. Still to stay away seemed impossible and she owed it to her Gramma to see that the new owners were good people. By all indications they were in fact very good people and very nice looking too. They moved in only one week ago and set forth decorating it with beautiful Christmas decorations. Gramma would be impressed, Leigh thought to herself as she gazed at the large wreath covered in frosted fruits and rich burgundy bows. Gold musical horns and notes were also tucked into the greenery of the wreath. Through the front window a large tree with hundreds of white lights twinkled and reflected on the many bows and balls that hung perfectly spaced apart. While the snow fell silently around once again Leigh remembered holidays gone by with Gramma Kate, mugs of hot chocolate, warm from the oven shortbread cookies. She remembered popcorn, popcorn and more popcorn, some to eat but most to string for the tree. Shaking her head and smiling, Leigh was startled when she felt a hand squeeze her shoulder. Quickly she turned but no one was there, she must have imagined it. Turning back to the house for one more look she realized that she didn't feel bad, she actually felt like she was in limbo, neither moving forward or back. Leigh didn't realize how long she stood there reminiscing as the evening drew on until again she was startled when she felt a pressure on her shoulder. This time it was her mother's hand as she turned her towards her.

"Leigh you gave me a scare. One minute you were in the house and the next you weren't. What are you doing here?" Jacqueline asked worry filling her eyes.

"Sorry Mom, it just got too noisy in there and I wanted a little quiet. I was just planning on going for a walk and I found myself here. It's really nice what they've done to the house isn't it?" Leigh asked.

"Yes it is," was all Jacqueline could reply with a lump forming in her throat. Putting her hand in her daughter's they turned and made their way back to their house with all the noise and all the life. As they walked up the driveway crunching the packing snow that covered the ground, Leigh stopped and pulled her mom into a tight hug.

"I miss her, Mom," she said into her mother's shoulder.

"I know Sweetheart, I miss her too," Jacqueline agreed and then pulled back to kiss her daughter's glistening cheeks. "Let's get some hot chocolate," she added knowing that Leigh wouldn't say no.

Leigh was outside cutting flowers for her mother, choosing only the very best of pinks and purples when she remembered the beautiful garden phlox her Gramma Kate grew. Intent on creating the best bouquet, Leigh headed over to her Gramma's to find what she needed. As usual she found her Gramma setting up her paints on her porch and Leigh sat down to join her. The wind was warm and sweet smelling from all the blooms; the sounds of birds and bugs were all around. Leigh could even smell her Gramma's favourite perfume; it was all so very real. Enjoying the afternoon Leigh painted and talked as she always did. Gramma left the porch for a few minutes returning with milk and cookies for the both to share like always. And like always they laughed and joked about their paintings. Quickly the scene seemed to speed up and Leigh found herself following her Gramma into her living room where they both stopped and stared at the oil painting of the laneway that had become so familiar to Leigh, only this time Leigh could see a couple walking down the centre of the lane and then everything went fuzzy. Leigh could hear the sound of her bedroom clock and the running of the shower down the hall. It was morning again. Sunday morning.

With only two weeks until Christmas Leigh had just a few days left of school. Usually there would be talk of family get-togethers and social events but this year there seemed to be little discussion on both ends. Jessie, a good friend of Leigh's, invited several friends to her parent's chalet for some skiing and the idea actually sounded really great to Leigh. Normally she would spend most of the holidays with Gramma Kate what with her family running off to hockey games and practices, work dinners and parties and shopping trips. Shopping trips were the best reason though, nothing practical when you went shopping with Gramma. Realizing that this time of the year would be difficult, Jacqueline made arrangements with Leigh to pick her up after school on Tuesday to start a new tradition. For Leigh it was bittersweet.

The next five days flew by, school was over for two weeks and Leigh and her mother had a great evening shopping and having dinner. The dreams still filled her nights but the days kept her mind mostly off of her loss as she was constantly kept in the thralls of holiday hullabaloo and hockey, hockey and more hockey. The house fluctuated from total quiet to busy and loud, but that was what the holidays were all about and as the house filled with laughter and excitement so did Leigh's heart. On Christmas morning within beautifully wrapped boxes she found several outfits, a new watch, some books and games and her mother had added to her art supplies with several canvases for her paintings. For only a brief moment did she allow herself to ache and then she pulled herself together knowing that her Gramma wouldn't want her to mourn endlessly. Besides, she was still seeing her every night as she dreamed and that was comforting, in fact the ending of the dream with them standing together by the painting continued to grow clearer and clearer every night. *Gramma was still nearby*.

Chapter Two

(From the Novel "Painted Dreams")

The weekend of the big ski trip had come and Leigh was going to spend the next three days at her friend Jessie's parents' chalet. Several classmates were also going to join them and Jessie's mother would stay with at the neighbouring chalet. Leigh packed lots of warm clothes, extra socks, gloves and toques. This would be the first time she was away from home for more than a night where she wasn't with family; she was nervous but excited as well. Her brother Mitch told her she could take his old skis and Jessie's mother had promised Jacqueline that she would make Leigh take an early one-hour lesson with an instructor before she joined the rest of the friends on the slopes. Everything was settled and all that remained was the giddy drive up with a group of energetic teens with dreams of good-looking skiers and late night games of truth or dare. As if to start the race the sound of honking could be heard from the driveway and the glow of flashing headlights shone through the front window. "They're here!" laughed Leigh as she grabbed up her weekend bag and launched herself towards her Mother who was standing in front of the closet.

"I know, I know. Remember to pay attention at the lesson, please be very careful. Have fun," Jacqueline managed to get out while being hugged and then loaded with gear while Leigh struggled to get her jacket and stuff on. Mark had been waiting in the garage so that he could load the skis on the roof rack with all the others. Leigh kissed her Mother once more, did the same as she passed her father outside beside the car and jumped into the back seat without skipping a beat! *Let the adventure begin,* she thought.

The car ride went much faster than Leigh thought it would but then again there was never a lull in the conversation for anyone to notice time. They stopped only once for drinks and a bathroom break and the group of girls laughed and sang and chattered their way all the way to the chalet. Jessie's mother was quite relieved when she made the final turn off the main road and drove back into the sugar bush towards the family get away. Get away indeed, she would need a few days rest to recuperate from the loud and excited drive up before she would pile that gaggle of girls back into her minivan. Everyone unloaded and took off into the chalet to claim their sleeping quarters. Some would have bunk beds, some would have couches and the unfortunate few would have to make due with air mattresses on the floor, but at least they were young and too excited to really care! With Leigh being the last one loaded she was the first unloaded and lucky to enter the chalet before anyone else and find the lower bunk of a set of bunk beds free. Jessie left her stuff behind but quickly went into the chalet and threw her jacket and pillow onto the upper bunk with a smile and a wink to Leigh. "First come, first served!" she announced with a conspirator slap on Leigh's back. It took the girls an hour to get settled in and another hour to discuss their plans for the next couple of days. They would start tomorrow with a big breakfast and after they would hit the slopes. Leigh would take her lesson while the other girls tried the different slopes, that way they could decide which one would be the best for her to run down after her lesson was over. *This group of girls are pretty nice,* Leigh thought, *for spending time on what would most likely be the smallest of hills out there.* She decided she would definitely encourage them to go on some of the bigger ones while she would take a break and watch. Evening snuck up quickly, as it usually does when you're having so much fun. The girls ordered three large pizzas fully loaded for dinner while they got ready to watch a movie. Jessie jumped up first and ordered the rest to change into their pyjamas and meet in the large living room on the main floor. It was like being inside a dryer, clothes were flying everywhere, pillows and other objects began to soar across the bedrooms and the hall as well and there was so much laughter and mumbling that all you could hear was a constant but load hum of noise. It was the best noise Leigh had heard in a long, long time. For a moment she thought about all the sleepovers she had had with Gramma Kate and although they were never this riley they always made her smile as much as she was now. *Shake it off*, she told to herself, and she did for the most part.

Falling into her bunk after hours of food, laughing and other girly stuff Leigh was exhausted. Her head barely hit her pillow before she was fast asleep and dreaming. Most of the night went by with typical bits and pieces playing in her mind...most that she would never even remember and then like always her dream began again. While it played out in her mind she was rolling around in her bunk and whimpering quietly. Hearing the muffled sounds coming from the bunk below her Jessie hung her head over the side to check on her friend. At first she thought that maybe Leigh had woken up in the middle of the night and was homesick but it didn't take her but a moment to realize that Leigh was fast asleep and having a very upsetting dream. Hesitating on whether or not to wake her up Leigh suddenly changed in attitude. Jessie watched with relief, as Leigh seemed to become calm and almost smiling at her dream now. *Good thing I didn't wake her*, Jessie thought and lifted her head back up to her pillow allowing sleep to return.

The next morning came and the sounds echoing in the chalet were loud and frantic and silly. Alive with anticipation the girls dressed and raced to the kitchen to begin their breakfast meal. Jessie was an early bird and decided that she would sneak downstairs earlier and start the bacon and the hash browns. With the oven on and the bacon sizzling it wasn't long for the aromas to fill the chalet and have all the others waking as well. Leigh was second on the scene and offered to make the toast while Angie arrived and took on the duty of scrambling the eggs. The entire process actually went smoothly and besides running short on bacon the group of girls were well fed and ready to start their day. Jessie's Mom entered the chalet just as the girls were cleaning the last few dishes. "Everyone ready then?" She asked already knowing the answer. The excited group called out a loud and resounding "Yes."

The lesson seemed to fly by and Leigh was not sure she actually learned anything but for some reason her instructor was having her follow him onto a lift and she was a bundle of nerves. The chair came around behind her and quickly she sat down grabbing tightly to the bar and her poles, unfortunately that was the easy part. As the chair carried her higher and higher she became more and more nervous and remembered why she never did anything even remotely sporty, but the time had come and she literally had to take that first leap. As her instructor was raising the bar and she stared at him in disbelief she watched the skiers ahead of her and couldn't believe that she was supposed to jump off the chair and land on a slope at the very top of the hill. What had she been thinking? Because of the fear and the inexperience when she jumped from the chair she landed flat on her back and had several younger skiers giggling at the sight. Fortunately being laughed at was not something that overly bothered her, as she was more grateful that she only hurt her pride and not anything physical. She stood up and brushed herself off and followed the instructor who was apologizing and asking her if she was all right. Of course she was, she smiled and nodded. The rest of the day went as planned, she made some good runs, she fell a lot and she watched with admiration at the group of friends that maneuvered over the hills with an aged practise that seemed perfect. Dinner was the same as the evening before because really how could one go wrong with pizza and snacks and so forth? Instead of a movie for the second evening the girls sat around talking about boys and school and all things pertaining to a teenager's life. When the topic turned to Christmas presents everyone listened intently to the others list, from there they would comment on whether they had the same or whether it was a good or bad gift and so on. When Leigh took her turn she mentioned all her presents and finished with the art canvases from her mother and Angie jumped in to ask if she painted.

"Well I spent a lot of time with my Gramma painting but

I haven't done anything for the last few months," answered Leigh feeling both sad as well as guilty. She shifted in her seat and smiled trying to mask her feelings, as they were not something she wished to discuss or focus on for that matter. As Angie's interest was more due to her brother's, she didn't notice Leigh's change in temperament and continued on with her suggestion. "Well if you ever want to do some painting my older brother Sam takes a class after school with Miss. Evans and he has some great stuff!" She announced proudly. The thought rolled around in Leigh's mind for a moment and she was actually surprised to find that it intrigued her. "Maybe I will," she decided out loud. And not for the first time this weekend did she wonder why she didn't spend more time with this group of girls who seemed so fun and friendly. Knowing them in school and spending time out of school was two very different past times and the latter of the two she had never considered too much before. This would have to change. And smiling again she listened to the next girl talk of CDs and movies, clothes and jewellery and so on.

A Wind's Embrace

I can feel you. I can taste you.
I can hear you whisper past.
The scents of life you bring to me
such gifts aren't long to last.

Your touch is often cold and strong:
a tear it draws from me.
And other times its feather light:
a warm embrace that's sweet.

So many faces do you bear,
and gifts for lovers keep.
This world would simply cease to live,
if ever you did sleep.

A gentle brush and lift of hair,
that makes me turn your way.
The warmest stroke upon my skin,
brings thoughts of careless days.

I watch your hand at work sometimes,
and with respect I yield.
The lightness as a bird's in-flight,
a driving snow that shields.

Such plays do you orchestrate:
the world is all your stage.
For dancing trees and singing leaves,
you tease, persuade or rage.

A rustle as you pass the woods,
the grasses I can hear.
Upon your back a bird's sweet call,
it travels far and clear.

A part of all our canvases,
you bring such colour forth.
Providing life with winged seeds,
the cycle you restore.

It is because of your great gifts,
that I can compromise.
When watching in your furious state,
the damage I despise.

And so it is to you I say,
"I will forever be
a lover of your temperament,
in every last degree!"

§

The Thoughtful Brush

A story told; a Painters tale.
In colourful strokes she builds in layers.
The scene is set from blue of sky
She chooses now for truth or lie.

Deception plays a willing part.
The eye is tricked, right from the start.
When adding depth with colours bold,
She changes how the story's told.

If light of hand and light of face,
the plot will read like peaceful grace
If dark of night and dark of shade,
the tale will bode of pensive days.

Deciding now, she paints the ruse,
selecting from her thoughtful views.
The hours pass but time is missed
'til ache of neck and arm is list.

The canvas breathes a heavy sigh
When swathed by cloth nigh on nigh.
In light of day, the mind's eye clears
the scene is set, the theme appears.

With final strokes the tale concludes.
Will it be clear? Will it elude?
The painter now smiles with knowing eyes
Her piece complete, will speak no lies.

For readers shall stand mere steps away,
And read the tale that's on display.

It's Over!